TWO DOZEN RED ROSES

Adapted from the Italian of
ALDO DE BENEDETTI

by
KENNETH HORNE

ENGLISH THEATRE GUILD LTD.
Ascot House, 52 Dean Street, London, W.1.

PRINTED IN GREAT BRITAIN BY THE WHITEFRIARS PRESS LTD.
LONDON AND TONBRIDGE

PRESS APPRECIATIONS

Illustrated London News: " An amusing story."

The Lady: " These amiably contrived goings-on."

Daily Express: " This gay play."

Sunday Dispatch: " Vastly amusing."

Liverpool Post: " Probably the cleverest thing of its kind since ' The Mask and the Face.' . . . The plot is delightfully ingenious and full of surprising twists. Really brilliant comic idea."

Daily Telegraph: " A continental frolic by Aldo de Benedetti neatly done into English by Kenneth Horne."

Midland Daily Tribune: " Two and a half hours of enjoyment . . . you should laugh a great deal."

News of the World: " A sparkling evening."

Evening News: " A piquant idea spun out with much deft and delicate manipulation."

Tit-bits: " A sparkling comedy."

South Western Star: " ' TWO DOZEN RED ROSES ' is keeping audiences chuckling at the Lyric Theatre."

Muswell Hill Record: " A really light and cheerful comedy . . . extremely funny situations."

Yorkshire Evening News: " Pithy, amusing dialogue."

Brighton Gazette: " Signor de Benedetti has got a new and delightful twist on things."

South London Observer: " Excellent entertainment."

Sunday Times: " A diverting evening."

Evening Standard: " An ingenious light comedy situation. Deft adaptation.

Times: " Amusing central situation."

Daily Herald: " Amiable, humorous."

Sunday Chronicle: " Sprightly adaptation."

Barnet Press: " Light, brisk comedy."

The Queen: " Amusing comedy."

Jewish Chronicle: " Some really amusing situations."

Liverpool Echo: " A most amusing comedy. Kenneth Horne has made a grand job of it. An ingenious plot contrivance. A shapely piece with much sparkle. Clever dialogue with which the comedy abounds."

Brighton Evening Argus: " Light, amusing and neatly woven."

Brighton Herald: " An amusing and original situation."

Yorkshire Post: " Cleverly adapted. Full of amusing situations."

Evening Post: " An ingenious plot."

Sydenham Gazette: " An enjoyable evening's entertainment. Amusing marital comedy."

Recorder: " Exceedingly diverting. I thoroughly enjoyed it."

Richmond Herald: " Trips along daintily to its unusual ending "

This play was presented by Alec L. Rea and E. P. Clift with Roy Limbert at the Lyric Theatre, London, on May 25th, 1949, with the following cast :—

BERNARDO	*Michael Yannis*
ROSINA	*Sally Rogers*
TOMASSO SAVELLI	*Michael Shepley*
MARINA VERANI	*Evelyn Laye*
ALBERTO VERANI	*Edwin Styles*

Directed by RICHARD BIRD

SCENES

ACT I

The living-room at the Veranis' house in Rome.   Midday.

ACT II

The same—mid-afternoon, ten days later.

ACT III

The same—late that evening.

TWO DOZEN RED ROSES

ACT I

SCENE : *The living-room at the* VERANIS' *house in Rome.*

R. *is a window. Back* R. *is a smaller window, and back* R.C. *French windows open out on to a balustraded terrace from which steps are supposed to lead down to a garden. Back* L. *is a diagonal recess in which is set an open archway leading off* R. *to bedrooms, etc., and* L. *to front door, etc. Down* L. *a swinging door leads to kitchen, dining-room, etc. Under the window* R. *is set a writing desk with telephone and table lamp. Back* R. *is an open book-case. Back* C. *is a cocktail cabinet and* L. *a radiogram. Over this, on the wall, is a mirror.* R.C. *is a couch with, before it, a low coffee table bearing periodicals, a cigarette box, etc. There is an easy chair* L.C., *a small easy chair down* R., *and two elbow chairs—one down* L. *and the other at desk.*

The room, tastefully furnished in a simple modern style, is supposed to be on the first floor.

It is midday with sunshine outside.

(*Curtain rises on an empty stage. A low whistle is heard, off. There is a pause, and the whistle, a little nearer now, is repeated. A slight pause, and the face of* BERNARDO *appears, very cautiously, at window back* R., *looks in at the room, and moves on* L.

Enter BERNARDO (F. W.). BERNARDO *is thirty, swarthy and very good-looking. He smiles almost incessantly and does not inspire confidence. He wears slacks and a short-sleeved, open-collared shirt. In his hand he carries a single purple tulip tied up with a few laurel leaves. He now halts warily at the open French windows and again emits the whistle. At a slight noise, off, he bobs back out of view.*

7

Enter ROSINA, L. ROSINA, *a maid, is twenty-five, small, dark, pretty, honest and pert. She wears uniform. She bustles in and moves purposefully towards archway.*)

BERNARDO (*appearing round doorway*). Psst!

ROSINA (*starts and halts*). Bernardo! (*Horrified.*) What are you doing here?

BERNARDO (*stepping into the room*). Well—the side-gate was open—so naturally I came up.

ROSINA (*very agitated*). But you mustn't! You'll get caught!

BERNARDO (*boastfully*). Pff! I never get caught!

ROSINA. You speak as if you make a habit of sneaking into other people's houses! (*Glances anxiously at archway.*) They'd be *fur*ious.

BERNARDO (*with a shrug—grinning*). What do they expect if they keep a pretty maid, who leaves the side-gate open?

ROSINA (*moving towards him—indignantly*). I *don't* leave it open. The *catch* is out of order. What do you *want*, anyway?

BERNARDO (*encircling her waist—meaningly*). Well . . .

ROSINA (*interrupting*). Never mind! I don't want to know what you want. (*Pushing him off.*) Please go away! I'm not interested.

BERNARDO (*plaintively*). What's happened to you, Rosina? Two nights ago, when you walked with me in the rain, you . . .

ROSINA (*interrupting*). That was entirely different. I was off duty, for one thing, and—and besides, it was dark. I couldn't see your face. There was no need to understand half the things you said.

BERNARDO (*hurt*). Well I've only brought you a flower. (*Proffers it.*) There's no harm in that, is there?

ROSINA. Oh! . . . well . . . (*Takes posy without enthusiasm.*) Thank you, Bernardo! Now please go!

BERNARDO (*sulkily*). You never think much of my flowers.

ROSINA. Oh, I like them all right, only . . . (*Breaks off.*)

BERNARDO. Only what?

ROSINA. Well, you can't expect a girl to get excited over flowers from *you*, can you?

BERNARDO. Why not from me? Are they any less beautiful because they come from me?

ROSINA. Of course not, but—you *deal* in flowers. You're a *fl*orist. It's—it's like a man with a butcher's shop bringing you a couple of kidneys every time you meet him.

BERNARDO (*indignantly*). In any case, I'm *not* a florist. I'm a floral artist. I don't just sell flowers—I com*pose* them.

ROSINA (*glancing anxiously at archway*). Sssh !

BERNARDO. I make them into *mess*engers—am*bass*adors—not *bunch*es. I don't tie up flowers. I pre*scribe* them. I make them *mean* something.

ROSINA (*imploringly*). Bernardo, *please !* She'll *hear* you !

BERNARDO (*indicating posy*). To you, no doubt, that's just a tulip done up with a bit of laurel.

ROSINA. Well, what else is it ?

BERNARDO. To anyone of any natural perception, a purple tulip can mean only one thing.

ROSINA (*cynically*). Love, I suppose, or passion, or something.

BERNARDO. But not just passion ! Starved, neglected, unrequited passion !

ROSINA. I see ! And what's the idea of the laurel ?

BERNARDO. That's for . . . (*Hesitates, then suddenly grins disarmingly.*) That's for perseverance.

(*They both laugh.*)

ROSINA (*taking him by the arms, turning him, urging him out*). All right ! But you *must* go now.

BERNARDO (*trying to kiss her*). Just one, then !

ROSINA (*firmly*). No, no, *no !*

(BERNARDO *shrugs and moves forlornly towards French windows.*)

(*Relenting*). Oh, very well ! (*Glances at archway, moves after him.*)

(*They embrace.* TOMASSO *is seen to pass window. Enter* TOMASSO, *French windows.* TOMASSO SAVELLI *is a dry, spare man in his early fifties. His manner is disillusioned and a trifle weary, but there is a twinkle in his eye. He wears a light lounge suit, and carries a hat and walking-stick. At sight of the lovers he shows no surprise but stands regarding them with faint amusement.*)

ROSINA, *facing* TOMASSO, *sees him, and begins to struggle in* BERNARDO'S *arms.* BERNARDO, *unaware, strives playfully to retain her.*)

(*Muttering fiercely.*) Let go! Let *go*, you fool!

(BERNARDO *glances over his shoulder and releases her abruptly. They both stand looking sheepish.*)

TOMASSO. The—er—the side-gate was open, so I came up this way.

ROSINA. Yes, Signor Savelli. It's—it's the catch.

BERNARDO (*with a nervous laugh*). Out of order!

TOMASSO. Ah! (*Moves into room.*)

BERNARDO. Will that be all then, Signorina?

ROSINA. Yes, Signor Bernardo, just the—er—just the wreath.

TOMASSO. Wreath?

ROSINA (*trying to look sad*). My—(*clears her throat*) my auntie.

TOMASSO. Dt, dt! I'm sorry. (*Looks at* BERNARDO.) Haven't I seen you before?

BERNARDO (*eagerly*). Oh, yes, Signor Savelli. I'm Bernardo—the floral artist.

TOMASSO. The what?

ROSINA. He keeps the flower shop next door.

TOMASSO. Ah, yes! I remember. (*Hands hat and stick to* ROSINA.)

BERNARDO (*laughing*). Yes. (*Hesitates awkwardly.*) Well . . .

TOMASSO (*very courteously*). Good-day, Signor Bernardo!

BERNARDO (*backing uncomfortably towards French windows*). Good day, Signor! Good day!

(*Exit* BERNARDO *by French windows.*)

(TOMASSO *seats himself on couch and picks up a magazine.*)

ROSINA. Shall I tell the Signora you're here?

TOMASSO (*faintly surprised*). Isn't Signor Verani in?

ROSINA. No. Was he expecting you?

TOMASSO. Well, I—rather expected him to be expecting me.

ROSINA. Then, perhaps he'll come back.

TOMASSO. Perhaps he will.

ROSINA. Meanwhile, shall I . . . ? (*Breaks off, indicating archway.*)

TOMASSO. No, don't disturb her, Rosina. I'll wait. (*Settles himself with magazine.*)

ROSINA. Yes, Signor ! (*Moves slowly towards archway, halts, hesitates, turns and comes back.*) Signor Savelli

TOMASSO (*absently*). Um ?

ROSINA (*haltingly*). Please . . . you won't say anything about . . . what you . . . what we . . . (*Breaks off.*)

TOMASSO (*with a kindly smile*). Don't worry, child !

ROSINA (*suddenly smiling*). Thank you, Signor ! (*Turns and walks briskly to archway.*)

TOMASSO. But, if I were you . . . (*Pauses.*)

ROSINA (*halting and turning*). Yes, Signor Savelli ?

TOMASSO. . . . I should get my mistress to have that catch repaired.

ROSINA (*incredulously*). Your mistress ?

TOMASSO (*with a note of asperity*). I said, " if I were *you*," Rosina.

ROSINA. Oh, I see what you mean. Oh, *yes*, Signor !

TOMASSO (*meaningly*). You never know what you might lose.

ROSINA (*in full agreement*). *Oo, I know !*

(*Exit* ROSINA, *by archway, and to* L.)

(*Almost immediately the phone begins to ring.*)

TOMASSO (*ignores the bell for a moment, then looks up and shouts*). Hi ! (*Continues with his magazine a moment longer, then suddenly rises, muttering irritably.*) Oh, blast them ! (*Goes to phone and lifts receiver.*) Yes ?—yes, who is it ?—Who ?—Can't hear you ! —What ?—I say I can't hear. . . . I'm sorry, Signora, but if you'd speak a little closer to the mouthpiece—and stop interrupting. . . . Eh ?—I say if you'd speak a little . . . (*Aside.*) Oh, my God ! (*Irascibly.*) Yes, this is the Veranis' house.—No, it is *not* Alberto.—It doesn't matter *who* I am. What do you *want* ?

(*Enter* MARINA, *archway, from* R. MARINA VERANI *is a very handsome and attractive woman of forty—mercurial, impulsive, intelligent and altogether charming—though not always the soul of logic. She wears a smart morning gown, and carries a railway guide. She enters briskly, and halts in some surprise upon seeing* TOMASSO.)

MARINA. Oh, hullo, Tomasso !

TOMASSO (*turns in relief*). Take this, will you ?

MARINA (*moving to phone*). Who is it ?

TOMASSO (*peevishly*). *I* don't know ! I don't know what the damn woman's talking about !

MARINA (*takes phone and speaks into it—very courteously*). Hullo ? (*Looking rather shaken,* TOMASSO *returns to couch and sits.*) Yes—Yes, this is Signora Verani. Oh, it's *you ! . . . What* extraordinary person, dear ?—Oh ! Oh, *him ?* (*Laughing.*) That was only Tomasso. He's a *very* old friend.—Oh, no, not really ! It's only his manner. What ? (*Laughs and turns to* TOMASSO.) She says " manners, not manner ! " (*Returns to phone.*) Well, it's all fixed. Yes, Alberto's consented. Not with a very good grace, still—he's consented.—Yes, Thursday evening ! I don't know, exactly. I was just going to look it up. (*Turns.*) Tomasso, be a dear and see what time the train goes !

(TOMASSO *rises and catches book as* MARINA *tosses it to him.*)

(*Continuing into phone.*) Of course it'll be a most *aw*ful rush, but that's half the fun, isn't it ?

TOMASSO. Does it matter *where ?*

MARINA (*turning to him.*) What ? Oh, didn't I say ? Er . . . (*Into phone.*) What was the name of the place, dear ? Oh, yes ! (*To* TOMASSO.) Cortina !

(TOMASSO *perches on* R. *arm of couch and begins to flip the pages of the guide.*)

(*Continuing meanwhile into phone.*) I can't *think* how I'm going to get everything done. There's Madame Roget, and my hair and the cleaners—and I simply must get . . . (*Eagerly.*) Oh, *are* you ?—Now ?—I wonder if I could come with you. (*Turns.*) What's the time, Tomasso ?

TOMASSO. Er . . . ! (*Fumbling for watch, accidentally shuts book.*) Oh, blast ! Now I've gone and lost the place. Ten past twelve ! (*Recommences his research.*)

MARINA (*into phone*). Well, I think I can manage it, dear. I *must have* some shoes.—You pick me up here, then. What ?— Yes, in about ten minutes.—All right, darling ! What ?—What time's the what ?—Oh, the train ! (*Turns.*) Have you got it, Tomasso ?

TOMASSO (*irritably*).   Give me a chance, Marina !

MARINA.   You're not very good-tempered this morning, are you ?   (*Into phone.*)   Well, I'll tell you about the train when I see you, dear.—Yes.   All right !—Good bye !   (*Hangs up.*) I don't wonder she found your manner a little odd.

TOMASSO (*still poring over book—grumblingly*).   I was all right when I came in.

MARINA (*going to him impulsively*).   Oh, poor Tomasso !   It is rather confusing for you, isn't it ?   (*Kisses him lightly on the side of the head.*)

TOMASSO.·   Who *was* that, anyway ?

MARINA.   Tina—my cousin.

TOMASSO.   Well, I don't like her.   (*Reading.*)   Roma—Padova —Calalzo—Cortina.

MARINA.   Oh, she's charming, really.   As a matter of fact, we've often thought she'd be very nice for you.

TOMASSO.   Don't be tiresome, Marina !

MARINA.   You should be married, you know.   It'd do you good.

TOMASSO.   Look !   I'm a confirmed bachelor.   You *know* I'm a confirmed bachelor, and, what's more, you know *why* I'm a confirmed   bachelor,   so . . .   (*Reading.*)   Roma—Bolzano— Dobbiaco . . .   (*Breaks off jabbing book.*)   What *is* all this ?

MARINA.   I'm going away, that's all.

TOMASSO (*blankly*).   Going away ?

MARINA.   Only for a holiday.

TOMASSO.   What for ?

MARINA.   What for !

TOMASSO.   Aren't you well, or something ?

MARINA.   Of course I'm well.

TOMASSO.   What's the idea, then ?

MARINA (*rather at a loss*).   Well—to have a good time, I suppose.   I want to dance and meet people and ski and skate and roll in the snow.

TOMASSO.   Why should you suddenly start wanting to roll in the snow ?

MARINA (*evasively*).   I don't follow.

TOMASSO (*forcefully*).   Marina—why should a person of your— maturity—be seized with such an unlikely impulse ?

MARINA (*looks at him thoughtfully, then*).   Do you really want to know ?

(TOMASSO *nods*.)

(*Impressively*).   Panic!

TOMASSO.   I beg your pardon?

MARINA.   Panic, Tomasso!   I've suddenly *realized* something. Come here.   (*Takes his hand and leads him to mirror*.)   What do you see?

TOMASSO (*becoming a little sentimental*).   I see what I shall always see, Marina.

MARINA.   What's that?

TOMASSO.   A girl of nineteen—fresh and beautiful—with life in her eyes, laughter on her lips—and the world at her feet.

MARINA.   You see a respectable woman of forty.

TOMASSO (*surprised at her frankness*).   Yes?

MARINA (*turning to him quite fiercely*).   Perhaps you don't know what it is to be a woman?

TOMASSO.   No, I can't say I . . .

MARINA.   A woman who has been happily married for twenty years.   Who has settled down to a quiet life of security and utter contentment.

TOMASSO.   What about it?

MARINA.   It's a terrifying thought.

TOMASSO.   Terrifying!   Why?

MARINA.   Because, as time goes on, I shall get more settled still.—*Next* year I may not *want* to roll in the snow.   (*Moves away from mirror*.)

TOMASSO.   Will that matter?

MARINA.   Of course it'll matter because then it'll mean that I've done with my youth.

TOMASSO.   Oh, nonsense!

MARINA.   I *must* be a little giddy and romantic at least *once* more, Tomasso, if only to show that I'm *not* getting stuffy.

TOMASSO (*pricking up his ears*).   Romantic, did you say?

MARINA.   Certainly!   That's the whole point.

TOMASSO.   What's Alberto going to think about that?

MARINA.   Alberto will not know.

TOMASSO (*in surprise*).   Isn't he going with you?

MARINA.   No.   I'm going with Tina.

TOMASSO (*goes to her—portentously*).   *Why* isn't he going?

MARINA.   Because he hates snow and doesn't like walking uphill.

TOMASSO. Then why select Cortina ?

MARINA. For the precise reason that Alberto hates snow and doesn't like walking uphill.

TOMASSO (*shocked*). Do you mean to tell me that you are deliberately leaving your husband behind so that you may—philander ?

MARINA (*a little impatiently*). Oh, Tomasso, don't be so pompous ! What harm is there in a little innocent dalliance—if it should come my way ?

TOMASSO. But it's not coming your way. You're seeking it out.

MARINA. I don't propose to do anything *wrong*, you idiot ! I only want to prove to myself that romance would still show up if it got the chance. It's a matter of self-respect.

TOMASSO. Well, I most emphatically do not approve.

MARINA (*vehemently*). Why *should*n't an honest woman have the comfort and reassurance of a little courtship as much as a—as much as any other sort of woman ?

TOMASSO. Don't talk nonsense !

MARINA. Haven't I the right to know whether I'm still attractive ?

TOMASSO. You know perfectly well you're attractive.

MARINA. What evidence is there ?

TOMASSO. Your husband's devotion, for one thing.

MARINA. That's habit.

TOMASSO (*stiffly*). And mine, for another.

MARINA. Ah ! It's all right, I suppose, if *you* court me, but if anybody *else* . . .

TOMASSO (*interrupting severely*). I do *not* court you, Marina. It's a gross misrepresentation of facts to say that I court you. I courted you until you were married—since then I've offered you nothing but my reverence and respect. And I will *not* look up your train. (*Throws book into chair* L.C. *and moves huffily away.*)

MARINA. Very well ! But I warn you, I'm going.

TOMASSO (*throws himself into couch and picks up a magazine*). Well—don't say *I* haven't warned *you* !

MARINA. Good heavens ! Anybody'd think the world was coming to an end ! I'm only going to a ho*tel* for a *fort*night.

TOMASSO. Marriages have been broken up in the back of a *taxi*-cab during a *traf*fic block, before now.

MARINA. Well, I can't stand here and argue all day. I've

got to go out. (*Goes up to archway, turns.*) Er—did you want anything, dear ?

TOMASSO. Want anything !

MARINA. I mean, did you come for any particular reason, or—(*Breaks off*).

TOMASSO. Yes—lunch !

MARINA (*surprised*). Did you ? (*Moves down to him.*)

TOMASSO (*not at all surprised*). Didn't you expect me ?

MARINA. I—I don't think *I* asked you, dear.

TOMASSO. No—Alberto did.

MARINA. Are you *sure* ?

TOMASSO (*fumbles for and produces a diary*). Of course I'm sure. Look ! (*Reading.*) "Monday, April the tenth. Lunch Veranis. Bolognese noodles ! "

MARINA. Oh, he *is* naughty !

TOMASSO. Forgotten, I suppose.

MARINA. He must have done. He's gone out, and there hasn't been a *word* about Bolognese noodles.

TOMASSO (*putting down magazine and beginning to rise*). Oh, well, then, I'll go and get something out.

MARINA (*urging him back*). No, please don't ! He *may* be back, and, anyway, *I* shan't be long. (*Moves up to archway.*)

TOMASSO. But, Marina, you know quite well that if I don't get my meals at the proper time (*putting his hand on his midriff*) my . . .

MARINA (*at archway—interrupting*). I know you're married to your stomach, Tomasso, but there's no need to let it wear the trousers. (*Smiles.*)

(*Exit* MARINA *through archway and to* R.)

(TOMASSO *shrugs faintly, picks up magazine and settles himself with an air of resignation. Almost immediately the phone begins to ring.*)

TOMASSO (*muttering*). Oh, my God ! (*Rises, goes to desk and grabs receiver.*) Yes ?—Who ?—Signor who ?—I can't get the name.—Golatti ?—Oh, Bogatti !—What ?—Well, *spell* it !—That's right, Bogatti !—That's what I said. What ? Oh, *not* Bogatti ? Well, never mind about your name. What do you want . . . ? Who ?

(*Enter* ALBERTO, *through archway, from* L.)

(ALBERTO VERANI *is a tall, good-looking man in his mid-forties. He is a sincere and charming person and is normally gay and confident in manner, but he is vain and easily " hurt " and at such times wears an air of boyish and not unattractive sullenness. He is dressed in a well-fitting lounge-suit. He enters briskly and halts in some surprise upon seeing* TOMASSO.)

ALBERTO.   Well, well, well !   Look who's here !

TOMASSO (*turning in relief*).   Oh, take this, will you ?

ALBERTO (*crossing*).   Who is it ?

TOMASSO.   Somebody whose name isn't Bogatti.

ALBERTO (*puzzled*).   *I*sn't Bogatti !   (*Takes phone and speaks into it.*)   Hullo ! . . . No, it is not.   (*Hangs up and turns with a smile.*)   We get a lot of that.

TOMASSO.   A lot of what ?

ALBERTO.   People wanting the little flower shop next door.

TOMASSO.   Bernardo ?

ALBERTO.   That's right !   Wires crossed or something !   (*Clapping* TOMASSO *affectionately on the shoulder.*)   Well, this *is* nice !

TOMASSO.   What is ?

ALBERTO.   You coming in like this.   Not in a hurry, are you ?

TOMASSO.   Hurry !   No, I . . .

ALBERTO (*interrupting*).   Have a drink, then !   (*Goes to cocktail cabinet.*)

TOMASSO (*takes out his watch and looks at it doubtfully*).   Well— I don't know whether I should—now.

ALBERTO (*dispensing two short drinks*).   Oh, a quick one won't hurt you.

TOMASSO.   It's past my time, you know.

ALBERTO.   Yes—I wondered what you were doing in this part of the world at this unwonted hour.

TOMASSO (*sourly*).   Actually, I understand I'm waiting for my lunch.   (*Sits* L.C.)

ALBERTO (*startled*).   Lunch !—you don't mean *here* ?

TOMASSO.   Yes, I do.

ALBERTO (*standing with the two filled glasses*).   I'm *terribly* sorry, old chap.   I didn't *know*.   She didn't say a word to me about it.   I only came *back* by chance.

TOMASSO (*wearily*).   Look !   We've *been* into all that, (*taking out his watch*) but if I don't get my . . .

ALBERTO (*interrupting*). You've *seen* her ?

TOMASSO (*putting watch away again*). Yes, she's . . .

ALBERTO (*interrupting*). Where *is* she, then ?

TOMASSO. Just going out.

ALBERTO (*incredulously*). *Just going out !* You don't mean she's for*got*ten ?

TOMASSO. Look, Alberto ! It'd save a lot of trouble if I came back another time.

ALBERTO. Not a bit of it ! I've got *some* sense of hospitality, you know. Here ! (*Thrusts a glass into* TOMASSO'S *hand.*) I'm not going to have you treated like that. I wouldn't mind betting she's even forgotten to order it. (*Strides to door* L., *opens it, and shouts.*) Rosina ! (*Turns back into room.*) I don't know what's the matter with Marina lately. Doesn't seem able to keep her mind on anything.

TOMASSO. This trip of hers, I expect.

ALBERTO. Oh, you heard about that, did you ? What do you think of it ?

TOMASSO (*weightily*). I don't like it, Alberto. I think you should do everything in your power to discourage it.

ALBERTO. What do you think I've been doing all the week ? (*Shouts.*) Rosina ! (*With sudden misgiving.*) *Why* don't you like it ?

TOMASSO (*uncomfortably*). Well, it's—unsettling.

ALBERTO. That's what *I* think.

TOMASSO. Especially for a woman—of her age.

ALBERTO (*faintly resentful*). What do you mean—" her age " ? She's younger than I am.

TOMASSO (*floundering*). Oh, I know, but . . . you know what I mean—women past their first flush of youth, and—er— (*Breaks off.*)

ALBERTO. What ?

TOMASSO. And—er—and yet still young enough to be attractive . . . (*Breaks off.*)

ALBERTO (*bemused*). What are you *talk*ing about ?

TOMASSO. They're apt to be a bit—impressionable.

ALBERTO (*in amused incredulity*). *What ?*

TOMASSO (*acutely uncomfortable*). And—and after living a rather humdrum sort of existence . . .

ALBERTO. Are you suggesting that I shouldn't trust my wife to be*have* herself ?

TOMASSO. Good Lord, no ! Of *course* I'm not !

ALBERTO. Well, what *do* you mean ?

TOMASSO. I only mean that—well—what with the holiday spirit and—so on—any woman's apt to get the least bit emotionally affected.

ALBERTO. But not Marina !

TOMASSO. You never know !

ALBERTO. Of *course* I. know ! I haven't lived with her for twenty years for nothing.

TOMASSO. That's just it, you . . .

ALBERTO (*interrupting*). No, no, old chap ! Don't go and spoil the market with *silly* arguments.

TOMASSO (*shrugging—miffed*). All right !

ALBERTO. Where *is* that brat ? (*Shouts.*) *Rosina ! !*

TOMASSO. Why don't *you* like it, then ?

ALBERTO (*wandering away* L.). Well, who's going to put out my underclothes and mix my hot drink and remind me about my pills, and . . . (*Breaks off as——*

ROSINA *enters* L.)

(*Turning to her*). Are you expecting Signor Savelli to lunch ?

ROSINA. No, Signor !

ALBERTO (*to* TOMASSO, *triumphantly*). There you are ! (*To* ROSINA.) Got anything in the house ?

ROSINA. No. I didn't even expect Signora Verani to be in.

ALBERTO. Well, pop round to the delicatessen or make an omelet or something, will you ? Only knock up something quickly, there's a good girl, because Signor Savelli's apt to get a pain.

(ROSINA, *with an expression of blended puzzlement and annoyance, withdraws* L.)

I'd have got in some Bolognese noodles for you, if I'd known.

(*Enter* MARINA, *through archway, from* R. *She is now smartly dressed for the street.*)

MARINA (*to* ALBERTO). Oh, good ! You're back ! (*Hurrying across.*) Tina there yet ? She usually toots.

ALBERTO (*a little coldly*). *No*body has tooted.

MARINA (*at French windows, glances obliquely to her right and turns away*). Dt! She's *never* on time!

ALBERTO. I suppose you know we have a guest?

MARINA. But I shan't be long, dear. I'm only going to look at some shoes.

ALBERTO (*sarcastically*). Snow-shoes?

MARINA (*laughing*). No, silly!

ALBERTO. Well, you've got thousands of every *oth*er kind.

MARINA. Darling, I must have *some*thing new to go away with.

ALBERTO. Why?

MARINA. Well—I want to look *nice*, don't I? That's half the fun of it.

ALBERTO. You're not going away simply in order to look nice, are you?

MARINA. No, of course . . .

ALBERTO (*interrupting*). Because you can look nice here as well as anywhere. There's no need to go all that way to do that.

MARINA (*patiently*). I only said it was *half* the fun, anyway.

ALBERTO. What's the other half, then?

MARINA (*rather at a loss*). Well, there's . . . well . . .

TOMASSO (*interposing*). All sorts of things.

MARINA. Alberto, *don't* let's start that all over again.

ALBERTO. *I'm* not starting anything again.

MARINA. We've got it *set*tled once.

ALBERTO. *Cert*ainly it's settled. (*Sits couch.*)

MARINA. Very well, then! (*Briskly.*) Now! (*To* TOMASSO.) What about a drink? Oh, you've got one.

ALBERTO. Tomasso thinks I should try to dissuade you.

MARINA (*with a resentful glance at* TOMASSO). Oh, he does?

(TOMASSO *avoids her eye.*)

ALBERTO. But I've said my say. You can't see my point of view—so that's that. You're going. I'm not going to say another word about it. (*Slight pause.*) I *should* rather like to know *why*, that's all.

(MARINA *rolls her eyes heavenwards, and turns away with a gesture of despair.*)

(*Appealing to* TOMASSO). That's not unreasonable, is it?

TOMASSO (*unhappily*). I wouldn't press the point, Alberto.

ALBERTO. But it's so damn silly! She's never been away from me before, and now, for no reason at all, she suddenly clears out for two whole weeks.

MARINA. I need a *change*.

ALBERTO. Nonsense! You're as strong as a horse.

MARINA (*trying to keep her temper*). I don't mean *physically*, dear—I mean *mentally*. I need—new *faces* for a bit.

ALBERTO. That's ridiculous. Rome's full of faces you've never seen in your life.

MARINE. A change of *scene*, Alberto!

ALBERTO. All right—so you want a change of scene! But why pick a climate that you know quite well will give you a red nose and chilblains, *both* of which you hate like *hell*?

MARINA. I needn't go *out*, need I?

ALBERTO (*appealing to* TOMASSO). You see? She says she needn't go out.

TOMASSO (*clears his throat*). Well . . .

ALBERTO (*interrupting*). She can't skate and she can't ski, yet she chooses a place where there's nothing but snow and nothing to do but skate and ski—that is, if there *is* any snow, which is doubtful half way through April.

TOMASSO (*tactlessly*). I wouldn't say there's nothing to do but skate and ski—even at Cortina.

MARINA. Well, you keep quiet!

TOMASSO. I'm only pointing out that there are always indoor games for the unathletic.

MARINA. If there's any pointing out to be done, *I*'ll do it.

ALBERTO (*morosely*). I only wish you would. (*Rising and going to cocktail cabinet—to* TOMASSO). Another?

TOMASSO. I daren't. (*Drains glass, rises, puts glass on coffee table, and returns to seat.*)

MARINA (*resentfully*). Anybody 'ud think you suspected me of an ulterior motive, or something.

ALBERTO (*refilling his glass*). I don't say an ulterior motive— but you must have darned sight better reasons than you've given so far.

MARINA (*losing patience*). And you want to know them?

ALBERTO. I'd like to—yes.

MARINA. Very well! (*Moves purposefully to* ALBERTO.)

TOMASSO (*anxiously*). Eh?

MARINA. If you're so anxious to . . .

TOMASSO (*interrupting hurriedly*). Er—didn't I hear some-body toot ?

MARINA. Oh, did you ? (*Runs up to French windows and looks out.*)

ALBERTO (*moving down to* R. *of chair* L.C.). I mean, if you *want* a change of faces . . .

MARINA (*interrupting—moving from window—to* TOMASSO). No, you did *not* hear anyone toot.

ALBERTO. I say, if you *want* a change of faces, for heaven's sake, why saddle yourself with one like Tina's ?

MARINA (*nearing the end of her tether*). Alberto, I don't care *whose* face it is.

ALBERTO. How d'you mean ?

MARINA. So long as . . . (*Breaks off.*)

ALBERTO. So long as what ?

MARINA. So long as it's not *yours !*

(TOMASSO *sits up.*)

ALBERTO (*gaspingly*). What ?

MARINA. Is *that* clear enough ?

ALBERTO (*stunned*). Do you—do you mean that you're deliberately going to—to get away from *me ?*

MARINA (*loudly*). *Yes !*

ALBERTO. But . . . (*Breaks off and feels behind him as if seeking the support of chair* L.C.)

TOMASSO (*hurriedly getting out of the chair and easing* ALBERTO *down into it—unhappily*). Look ! I'm *sure* I heard somebody toot !

(*The* OTHERS *ignore him.*)

MARINA (*her anger already subsiding*). *Now*, I suppose, you'd like an explanation of *that*.

ALBERTO (*pathetically trying to be dignified*). Thank you ! I—I think I should.

TOMASSO (*moving up* R.—*uncomfortably*). Well, I—think I'll just go and—keep an eye cocked for, erm . . .

(*Breaks off and removes himself discreetly through French windows on to terrace.*)

MARINA (*moves impulsively to behind* ALBERTO'S *chair, leans over it and encircles his neck*). Darling, I'm so sorry. I didn't mean to be brutal.

ALBERTO (*deeply wounded*). That's all right.

MARINA. I only meant that—that—well, we've been together so long that—I think we've grown a little used to each other.

ALBERTO. I can't see that that matters.

MARINA. It does matter, dear, because, you see, we don't *thrill* each other as much as we used to, and if we're not careful we shall lose the element of romance altogether—and we don't want to do that, do we ?

ALBERTO (*huffily*). I'm sorry to hear I don't thrill you as much as I used to.

MARINA (*straightening up—reasonably*). Well, you can't be expected to, dear. After all—we're neither of us as young as we were.

ALBERTO. No—I suppose not.

MARINA (*moving away* R.). And I thought it might help a little if we could get away from each other for a bit—every now and again—that's all. (*Sits* L. *arm of couch.*)

ALBERTO (*with a note of alarm*). Every now and again ? Am I to understand that you propose to make a habit of it ?

MARINA. Well, if it's a success this time, there's no reason why I shouldn't do it whenever it seems to be necessary, is there ?

ALBERTO. None at all ! May I ask what is meant by " a success " ?

MARINA. If we find we miss each other as much as I hope we shall, dear.

ALBERTO. I see.

MARINA. And come back to each other with—with a sort of renewed zest.

ALBERTO. In other words—if you find that it stimulates the ardour which—due to my increasing age and flagging charms— can no longer be achieved in any other way !

MARINA (*striving for patience, rises and moves behind couch*). *No*, dear, I don't mean anything of the *sort ! Please* don't be touchy. I'm merely suggesting something that *thou*sands of couples do as a matter of *rou*tine—as a pre*cau*tion—because they think it's *good* for them, like—like *ex*ercise or Epsom *salts* or something.

ALBERTO (*distantly*). There's no need to expatiate, my dear. It's all perfectly clear.

MARINA. I thought you *wanted* an explanation.

ALBERTO. I didn't quite appreciate the extent of my romantic deterioration, that's all.

MARINA. But it's not yours en*tirely*, dear. It's mine as . . .

ALBERTO (*interrupting*). *I* know. *I* know.

MARINA (*going to him*). Well, d'you see what I mean *now ?*

ALBERTO. Perfectly well !

MARINA. And you think it's worth trying ?

ALBERTO (*bitterly*). Of course ! Anything for a matrimonial dose of salts.

TOMASSO (*moving into room—interrupting*). I think she's . . . (*Indicates street.*)

(*A hooter is heard, off.*)

MARINA. Yes, there she is. (*To* ALBERTO.) We'll say no more about it, then—eh ? (*Kisses him on top of the head and goes up to archway.*) Oh !—I forgot to tell Rosina about lunch. See to it, will you dear ?

(MARINA *smiles, and exits through archway, to* L.)

(ALBERTO, *the glass still in one hand, remains staring blankly into space.*)

TOMASSO (*looks at* ALBERTO *for a moment, takes out watch and regards it with some anxiety, then wanders to French windows and looks down into street*). So that's Tina ! Well, *that* face will certainly make a change ! Though I shouldn't call it a new one, exactly—would you ?

ALBERTO (*absently*). Eh ?

TOMASSO (*moving towards couch*). Tina's face ! I say I shouldn't call it a . . . Oh, never mind ! (*Sits on couch and regards* ALBERTO *cynically.*)

(*There is silence for a moment.* ALBERTO, *sunk in anxious thought, is holding his glass at a rather precarious angle.*)

You'll spill that if you're not careful.

ALBERTO (*turns his head uncomprehendingly to* TOMASSO). Spill it ?

TOMASSO (*indicating glass*). That !

ALBERTO. Oh! (*Drains glass, rises, goes up to cabinet, deposits glass and remains standing sunk in thought.*)

TOMASSO (*after slight pause*). Alberto!

ALBERTO (*without looking up*). Um?

TOMASSO. You know—I can't help feeling that I've come at an awkward time.

ALBERTO (*without the least comprehension*). You don't say so!

TOMASSO. And I'm *sure* it would be *much* better if I just . . . (*Trails off as——*

ALBERTO *suddenly moves to mirror and begins peering at his face, viewing it from various angles and with different expressions. TOMASSO watches with growing wonder. After a few moments of anxious scrutiny, ALBERTO moves a little away and tries the effect of himself in a variety of positions. Finally, in trying to see himself in profile, he catches TOMASSO's eye, double takes him, looks a little sheepish, and moves away.*)

ALBERTO. What were you saying?

TOMASSO (*a little irritably*). What's the *matter* with you?

ALBERTO. I'm sorry. I'm a little preoccupied about something.

TOMASSO. But what were you staring at yourself like that for?

ALBERTO (*hesitates*). Come here a moment!

TOMASSO. Eh?

ALBERTO (*moves to* TOMASSO *and takes his arm*). Would you mind?

TOMASSO (*rising, wonderingly*). Why, what's . . .

ALBERTO (*interrupting*). Tomasso—you're an old friend—and you're an honest man. (*Puts his arm about* TOMASSO's *shoulders*) and I want you to tell me something. (*Moves with* TOMASSO *to confront mirror.*) I want you to be perfectly frank—brutal, if you like—but I want the truth. Now tell me . . .

TOMASSO (*interrupting—puzzled*). Haven't we done this once already this morning?

ALBERTO (*bemused*). What?

TOMASSO. Oh, no, no, of course not! I get a bit confused when my st . . .

ALBERTO (*interrupting plaintively*). Look! Don't play the fool, old man! I'm *serious*.

TOMASSO (*indignantly*). I'm *not* playing the fool. I *do* get confused when my stomach's empty.

ALBERTO. Well, I can't do more than order lunch, can I ?

TOMASSO. Yes, you can ; you can let me go *out* and have some, instead of getting all pompous about your idiotic hospitality. (*Turns away.*)

ALBERTO (*pleadingly*). Tomasso ! I'm telling you that I want your opinion on something *vital*—and you stand there and talk about your *stom*ach !

TOMASSO (*returning to him*). Oh, all right ! What is it ?

ALBERTO. Now, look here ! Look in that mirror and tell me what you see. Be quite objective about it. Pretend you've never seen that man before. Imagine yourself a stranger. Anyone. Say you're just a—well, a young woman in the street.

TOMASSO. Eh ?

ALBERTO. How would he strike her ?

TOMASSO. Strike her ?

ALBERTO. What would she think ?

TOMASSO (*considers, looking at* ALBERTO *in mirror*). Well, I don't know. I imagine she'd very likely think " I don't like the way that fellow's looking at my legs."

ALBERTO. No, seriously ! What impression would he make on her ?

TOMASSO (*considering reflection*). Oo ! Quite an agreeable one, I dare say.

ALBERTO (*eagerly*). You think so ?

TOMASSO. Yes. It depends what sort of a girl it is, I suppose —but the average one would probably say to herself : " Here comes a—presentable . . . (*Pauses, considering.*)

ALBERTO. Yes ?

TOMASSO. . . . well-dressed . . . (*Pauses.*)

ALBERTO. Yes ?

TOMASSO. . . . well-preserved person . . . (*Pauses.*)

ALBERTO (*startled*). Eh ?

TOMASSO. . . . of middle years.

ALBERTO. No, no, Tomasso ! Don't be such an egotist ! I'm talking about *me*, not *you !*

TOMASSO (*indignantly*). So am *I* talking about you.

ALBERTO (*quite horrified*). But—but you couldn't call me " well-preserved " !

TOMASSO. Well—aren't you ?

ALBERTO. But, I mean—you can't apply a word like " pre-*served* " to a chap like *me!*

TOMASSO. Why not ? You're forty-six.

ALBERTO (*staring*). *Am* I ?

TOMASSO. And you might easily be bald-headed and pot-bellied at that age. You ought to be very grateful that you're not.

ALBERTO (*unable to believe his ears*). Grateful that I'm not *pot-bel*lied ?

TOMASSO. Certainly ! I am.

ALBERTO. What ? Pot-bellied or grateful ?

TOMASSO. Grateful that I'm *not !*

ALBERTO. Yes, but that's different.

TOMASSO (*resentfully*). Oh, is it ?

ALBERTO. You're *older* than I am.

TOMASSO. Only five years, my friend.

ALBERTO (*startled*). *Are* you ?

TOMASSO. That's all—if you work it out.

ALBERTO (*staring at him, appalled*). Good Lord ! So it is !

TOMASSO (*going to coffee table and picking up glass*). So now you can take a look at *me* and laugh *that* off. (*Goes deliberately up to cabinet and, rather defiantly, pours himself out another drink.*)

ALBERTO (*sinks into chair* L.C., *looking grave—pauses slightly*). Funny thing, you know—I didn't realise, but I suppose I am.

TOMASSO. What ? (*Moves downstage with drink.*)

ALBERTO. Well—middle-aged !

TOMASSO (*with satisfaction*). You are !

ALBERTO. It sort of—sneaks up on you, doesn't it ?

TOMASSO (*sitting on couch—callously*). And what's more—before you know it you'll be saying " Elderly ? "—" What do you mean, elderly ? I'm only middle-aged ! " (*Takes a cigarette.*)

(ALBERTO *stares at him sourly, but makes no comment.*)

(*Lights cigarette.*) Then it'll be, " Senile ?—what do you mean, senile ? "

ALBERTO (*resentfully*). You know—anybody'd think you take a *plea*sure in talking like that.

TOMASSO. Getting old's no more pleasure for me than it is for you, I can assure you.

ALBERTO. I dare say, but it doesn't matter so much, does it ?

TOMASSO. Why not ?

ALBERTO. Well, you're a bachelor.

TOMASSO. What's that got to do with it ? We're human, aren't we ? Our teeth and hair drop out as much as a married man's, don't they ?

ALBERTO. Yes, but . . . (*Hesitates.*)

TOMASSO. We've as much to lose as you have, haven't we ?

ALBERTO. No—you haven't got wives to lose.

TOMASSO (*sitting up*). Eh ?

(*Telephone bell begins to ring.*)

ALBERTO (*rising—irritably*). Oh—*now* what ? (*Crosses to desk, lifts receiver.*) Hullo !—What ?—Who ?—Countess Arduini ?—Who do you . . . ? (*Light dawns.*) Oh ! (*Suddenly ironically ingratiating.*) Oh, *yes*, Countess, we have *hun*dreds of red roses. . . . Oh, with *pleasure* !—Two dozen, Countess ? Certainly ! Where would you like them sent ?—Via Guittone d'Arezzo twenty-two !—Of *course*, Countess, immediately ! I'll see to it myself.—Yes.—*Thank* you, Countess, *thank* you.—*Good* morning ! (*Replaces receiver and turns.*) That'll teach the fool !

TOMASSO. What's the idea ?

ALBERTO. She can sit and *wait* for her blasted red roses !

TOMASSO. I can't see that it's *her* fault if your wires are crossed.

ALBERTO (*crossing*). There's no need to take it for granted that I'm a flower shop, though.

TOMASSO. No—still . . . ! Did you say Countess Arduini ?

ALBERTO. Yes. (*Halts* L.C.) Why ? D'you know her ?

TOMASSO. I know her by sight. She's one of the loveliest creatures in Rome.

ALBERTO (*about to sit* L.C., *checks himself*). What—*that* ? (*Indicating phone.*)

TOMASSO (*impressively*). I once followed her for two miles and three quarters.

ALBERTO. *You* did ? What for ?

TOMASSO (*with dignity*). Simply because I was unable to take my eyes off her. She has the face of a Madonna.

ALBERTO (*sitting*). She must have something more than the face of a madonna to make you walk all that distance—unless she was walking backwards

TOMASSO. She has indeed. A good deal more. She was an artist's model at one time.

ALBERTO (*interested*). A model, eh? You don't mean in the—er . . . (*Breaks off delicately, making descriptive curving motions with his hands.*)

TOMASSO. I believe so—yes!

ALBERTO (*increasingly intrigued*). Go on! (*Glances at phone.*) She *had* rather a pleasant voice—come to think of it.

TOMASSO. That was before she married the count, of course.

ALBERTO. Well, naturally!

TOMASSO. Poor kid!

ALBERTO. Why " poor kid "? She seems to have done pretty well for herself.

TOMASSO. Oh, he's an awful swine!

ALBERTO. Who, old Arduini?

TOMASSO. Oh, he's a shocker!

ALBERTO. You mean he knocks her about, or something?

TOMASSO. Oh Lord, yes—leads her a hell of a life.

ALBERTO. What a shame! (*Slight pause.*) Bit of a dirty trick really, you know!

TOMASSO. What?

ALBERTO. Well—letting the poor little devil think she's going to get her flowers.

TOMASSO (*in agreement*). Well, I must say . . .

ALBERTO (*suddenly rises*). Look! *I* know what I'll do. (*Goes to phone, lifts receiver, dials.*) Makes you sick to think of a sweet little thing like that and a great hulking brute of a . . . (*Breaks off and speaks into phone.*) Hullo! Is that Bernardo? Look—do you know Countess Arduini?—That's right, number twenty-two. She wants some red roses. Have you got any?— Well, send her round a couple of dozen, will you?—What?—It doesn't matter who I am. I'm only giving a message.—Well, charge 'em up to *her*, I suppose! No—charge 'em to the Count! —See to it at once, will you?—All right! Thanks! (*Hangs up.*) How long has Marina been gone?

TOMASSO (*takes out his watch*). Six minutes and twenty-five seconds.

ALBERTO. Because *I*'m getting *hung*ry, you know. (*Crosses to* L.C.)

TOMASSO (*murmuring sarcastically*). That's too bad!

ALBERTO (*notices railway guide in chair* L.C., *picks it up*). Next thing, I suppose, she'll be wanting me to look up a train for her. (*Throws book down again.*) Do you know *why* she's going away ?

TOMASSO (*evasively*). Do you ?

ALBERTO. Yes. Because I'm beginning to pall on her. (*Begins restlessly to pace the room.*)

TOMASSO. How d'you mean ?

ALBERTO (*bitterly*). It seems I've reached an age when I no longer appeal to her senses. So I'm to be abandoned for a succession of fortnights on the theory, apparently, that absence makes the heart grow fonder.

TOMASSO. Is *that* what she told you ?

ALBERTO. Words to that effect.

TOMASSO. I see. (*Indicating mirror.*) Hence all this— posturing !

ALBERTO. Well, I wanted to see what she meant.

TOMASSO. And did you ?

ALBERTO (*rather pathetically*). No, I can't say I did. (*Pauses before mirror.*) I look all right to me. (*Resumes pacing.*)

TOMASSO (*sourly*). Well, that's all right then, isn't it ?

ALBERTO. No, because, the point is—what do other people think ?

TOMASSO. Other women, you mean ?

ALBERTO (*self-consciously*). Well—yes—if you like. I mean, if I *have* lost my, er . . . If I'm not so sort of . . . Well, I'd like to *know*, that's all.

TOMASSO (*getting bored*). Naturally !

ALBERTO. It's—it's the un*cer*tainty of it.

TOMASSO (*absently*). Quite !

ALBERTO (*resentfully*). It's most un*fair* of her to say a thing like that because there's *no* way of dis*prov*ing it.

TOMASSO. No.

ALBERTO (*halting*). Unless, of course . . . You know—it 'ud serve her right if I went off and sought reassurance elsewhere.

TOMASSO. Yes. (*Suddenly coming to—turning his head.*) What are you *talk*ing about ?

ALBERTO. A fortnight's freedom would be a heaven-sent opportunity to many husbands, you know.

TOMASSO (*rising*). Now, look here . . .

ALBERTO (*interrupting—pacing again*). Come to think of it— the most *hurt*ful thing about the *whole* business is the *blind* way she *trusts* me. It never enters her *head* that I might have a bit of fun while she's away.

TOMASSO. What's wrong with trusting you ? *You* trust *her*.
You said so.

ALBERTO. That's different. Women ex*pect* to be trusted.
But *I'm* a *man*—a member of the sex which is no*tor*iously un-
reliable in that respect. Why should she take it for granted
that I can be left *all* that time without a *mo*ment's anxiety.
Why ?

TOMASSO (*testily*). *I* don't know.

ALBERTO. Obviously, my dear chap, because she thinks I'm
no longer pleasing enough to get anyone's co-operation. (*Halts
at cabinet and begins to pour another drink.*)

TOMASSO (*getting bored again*). All right ! You've got all
that worked out ; now what are you going to do about it—have
your face lifted ? (*Moves down* R.)

ALBERTO. No, but she'd only have herself to blame if I *did*
have a slap at disproving it. (*Takes a gulp at his drink.*)

TOMASSO (*rather wearily*). Well, you know you won't—so why
harp on it ?

ALBERTO (*fiercely*). I don't know I won't at all ! (*Takes
another gulp.*) What's to prevent me from starting something
with—well, this young Countess, for instance ?

TOMASSO (*sitting, down* R.). Only the Count !

ALBERTO. You don't think I should be afraid of a rat like
that, do you ?

TOMASSO. I should be.

ALBERTO. Oh, you *would ?* (*Gulps the rest of his drink, puts
down glass and walks purposefully to desk.*) Well, I haven't
reached the stage *yet* that I'm to be intimidated by elderly and
bad-tempered noblemen. (*Lifts receiver and dials.*)

TOMASSO (*sitting up, faintly alarmed*). *Now* what are you up
to ?

ALBERTO. You'll see.

(TOMASSO *rises, goes to* ALBERTO, *and stands watching
apprehensively.*)

(*Into phone.*) Hullo ! Bernardo ?—Have you sent off those
roses to the Countess Arduini yet ?—Good ! Well, don't !—No,
send them up here—next door !—That's right, Signor Verani !—
What ?—Yes, it was me.—No, don't come to the front door ;
bring 'em up the side way. I think you'll find you'll be able to
get in. The catch is out of order.—Oh ! you know !—Yes, right

away, will you ?—Thanks ! (*Hangs up.*) I'll show her ! (*Sits at desk and begins searching in a drawer.*)

TOMASSO (*portentously*). Alberto ! What—are—you—doing ?

ALBERTO. I'm starting a courtship, that's all.

TOMASSO. You're *what ?*

ALBERTO. And to put the wheels in motion, I'm sending the roses myself. (*Finds a card.*) Ah !

TOMASSO. Have you gone in*sane ?*

ALBERTO. No. This little Countess of yours will do as well as anyone else—perhaps better, if what you say about her is true. (*Picks up pen.*) After all, if I'm going to do it at all, I might as well enjoy myself. (*Considering.*) Now, let me see !

TOMASSO (*severely*). Would you be good enough to recall the fact that you're a married man ?

ALBERTO. Look ! I've been faithful to my wife for twenty years, and I intend to remain so. (*Considering.*) Erm !

TOMASSO. Then what are you playing at ?

ALBERTO. All I want the girl to do is to mistake my intention as *you*'re doing—and *like* it. (*Considering.*) Each petal is a . . (*Breaks off and begins writing.*)

TOMASSO. Well, all I can say is . . .

ALBERTO (*interrupting*). Do shut up a minute, old man ! I'm trying to com*pose* something.

(TOMASSO *moves huffily away, drops into chair* L.C., *whips out his little bottle and takes two pills.*)

Each petal . . . Each petal is a . . . Now what would each petal be ? (*Writing.*) . . . word of love . . .

(BERNARDO'S *grinning face appears at window, up* R., *looks in and passes on. Enter* BERNARDO (F. W.). *He carries a large bunch of red roses.*)

BERNARDO (*halting cautiously in doorway*). Pssst !

ALBERTO (*looks round*). Oh, there you are !

BERNARDO (*with the air of a conspirator*). Is it all right ?

ALBERTO. Yes, yes of course it's all right. Put 'em down here, will you ? (*Indicates desk.*)

BERNARDO (*going to desk*). They're very beautiful ones, Signor. (*Holds flowers to* ALBERTO'S *face.*) Smell !

ALBERTO (*recoiling slightly*). Very nice !

BERNARDO (*with a leer*). *She* will love them. (*Puts flowers on desk.*)

ALBERTO (*coldly*). Yes—well, that'll be all for the moment. (*Turns back to his card.*)

BERNARDO (*backing to* F.W.). Thank you, Signor! Any time, you know. You can always rely on Bernardo.

ALBERTO. Good-morning.

BERNARDO (*in doorway*). Do I still charge them to the Count?

ALBERTO (*without looking up*). Er—no, put 'em down to me!

BERNARDO. Ah! (*Laughs impurely.*) Good-morning, Signori!—Any time!

(*Turns, looks cautiously right and left outside and leaves,* F.W.)

ALBERTO. You know—I don't think I like that chap.

TOMASSO. Seems to have *you* pretty well taped.

ALBERTO (*writing—muttering*) . . . tery man! (*Blots card, picks it up, rises, crosses and hands it with some pride to* TOMASSO.) How's that?

TOMASSO (*examines card a moment*). And is this school girl slop what you call putting the wheels in motion?

ALBERTO (*resentfully*). What's the matter with it?

TOMASSO. My *dear* fellow. (*Reads with extreme distaste.*) "Each petal is a word of love—Mystery Man." (*Grimaces.*)

ALBERTO (*looking foolish*). Well, women *like* that sort of thing.

TOMASSO. This is a *decent* woman, Alberto.

ALBERTO. *All* women have a chink in their armour.

TOMASSO. And *printed*—like an anonymous letter—or something written on the wall by nasty little boys!—How strangely unpleasant, Alberto!

ALBERTO. But that helps to make it mysterious.

TOMASSO. What, block letters?

ALBERTO. Yes.

TOMASSO. Must it be mysterious as well as all the other things it is?

ALBERTO. Of course! You've obviously got to intrigue the woman first. You can't just bust in on her.

TOMASSO (*grimacing*). But—"Mystery Man"! (*Hands card back.*)

ALBERTO. Well, that's all part of the same thing.

TOMASSO. Intriguing her?

ALBERTO. Certainly!—Now, listen! (*Getting explanatory,*

begins pacing.) She gets a bunch of red roses. Right! At first she thinks the florist has sent them.

Tomasso. Not unnaturally—considering she ordered them herself !

Alberto. Quite! But then she opens them and finds this. (*Indicates card.*) What happens ?

Tomasso. She's sick on the floor !

Alberto. No—she's *cu*rious. That's inevitable. She says to herself : " Who *is* this man—what *sort* of a man is he ? "

Tomasso (*muttering*). I'm beginning to wonder myself.

Alberto. To-morrow she gets another bunch with another note.

Tomasso. Uh ?

Alberto (*reasonably*). Oh, yes! I can't expect her to fall into my arms just on the strength of *this !* (*Indicates card.*)

Tomasso. You're too humble.

Alberto. And the next day another—and so on !

Tomasso. How long does this go on ? You've only got a fortnight, you know.

Alberto. Only until she shows she's ready to play.

Tomasso. And how's the poor little brute supposed to do that ?

Alberto (*halting*). Eh ?

Tomasso. Well, there's no address on that thing. (*Indicates card.*)

Alberto. Oh! (*Considers.*) Well, that's easy enough. (*Goes to desk, sits, begins writing on card—muttering.*) If—they—please —you—put—them—in—your—window. (*Blots card, rises.*) There you are ! Each time the same footnote.—(*Reads.*) "" If they please you, put them in your window ! " (*Puts card in flowers—expounding again.*) Now, to continue ! After a day or so a certain uneasiness sets in. She begins to ex*pect* the flowers— to wait for them. She's irritated and, at the same time, fascinated Who *is* this " Mystery Man " ? By degrees he becomes an ob*sess*ion. She's *haun*ted by him.

Tomasso. I can believe that part.

Alberto (*flourishing flowers*). She looks for him in the faces of her friends. She spies from her window. She jumps at every ring of the bell. The thought of him *dom*inates her, and yet— nothing ! Only the notes and the flowers—until she can bear it no longer !—So, one day—perhaps the second—perhaps the third—perhaps the tenth—they appear in her window.

TOMASSO (*having furtively consulted his watch again*). Of course, if you're giving up any idea of lunch, just say so and I'll do my best to forget it.

ALBERTO (*crossing to him—with concern*). It *isn't* good for you, is it—all this hanging about ?

TOMASSO (*surprised*). No, it isn't !

ALBERTO (*kindly*). Well then, why don't you just pop out and get something, old chap ?   We shall quite understand.

TOMASSO. Uh ?

ALBERTO. And while you're about it—perhaps you'd just drop these in at number twen . . .

TOMASSO (*interrupting*). *Oh*, no you don't !   (*Rises.*)

ALBERTO. But . . .

TOMASSO (*interrupting*). No !   No !   Absolutely and definitely *no !*—I'd rather stay to lunch.

ALBERTO. It wouldn't take you far out of your . . .

TOMASSO (*interrupting*). You can do your *own* dirty work.—I'll have no part in it.

ALBERTO. But you can't expect *me* to do it.   Supposing the Count opened the door !

TOMASSO. I thought you weren't afraid of the Count.

ALBERTO. I'm *not*, but I should look such a *fool*.

TOMASSO. It doesn't *matter* if *I* look a fool, I suppose.

ALBERTO. All right !   I'll get Bernardo to do it.   (*Deposits flowers on coffee-table, goes up to phone, lifts receiver, dials.*)

TOMASSO (*with an anxious glance at archway*). Meanwhile, hadn't you better get those things out of the way ?   (*Indicates flowers.*)

ALBERTO. Oh, she'll be ages yet.

TOMASSO. Then, for God's sake give me a dry biscuit or something !

ALBERTO (*into phone*). Hullo !   Bernardo ?—Oh, Signor Verani again !   Look !   Come up and get those flowers, will you ?   I want you to deliver them.—Right !   (*Hangs up and moves* L.)   All right !   Come on !   We'll see what we can find. (*At door* L.)   I thought you didn't like dry biscuits.

(*Exit* ALBERTO L.)

TOMASSO (*following*). I don't, *per*sonally !   I'm speaking on behalf of my duodenum.

(*Exit* TOMASSO L.)

(*There is a slight pause and* MARINA *is seen to pass window up* R,

Enter MARINA (F.W.). *She looks round expectantly, registers faint surprise at seeing nobody, moves down and begins to pull off her hat. The action is arrested as she sees the flowers. She stares at them curiously for a moment, then continues taking off her hat, puts it on back of couch and, wearing a little puzzled frown, moves round to* R. *of coffee-table.*

Enter ROSINA L.)

ROSINA (*halts on seeing* MARINA). Oh, you're back! I didn't hear the bell.

MARINA (*interrupting*). No. I came in the side way. The catch is out of order.

ROSINA. Yes, I . . . (*Checks herself.*) Oh, is it ?—What lovely flowers ! (*Continues on towards archway.*)

MARINA. Yes. Where did they come from ?

ROSINA (*halting*). Didn't you bring them ?

MARINA. No.—Weren't they delivered ?

ROSINA. No, Signora ! (*Comes down to* L. *of coffee-table.*)

MARINA. But . . . (*Breaks off at a loss.*)

ROSINA. Perhaps the Signor . . . !

MARINA. He's never done such a thing in his *life*, Rosina.

ROSINA. Well, I know it wasn't Signor Savelli, because I was—(*looks a little sheepish*)—I was here when he came.

MARINA. But somebody must have . . . Are you *sure* nothing was delivered ?

ROSINA. Positive, Signora ! I should have heard the bell even if one of the gentlemen had taken them in.

MARINA. Well—what an extra*or*dinary thing !

ROSINA (*struck by a thought*). You—you don't think anybody could have . . . ? (*Breaks off and glances at French windows.*) I mean, if the catch *is* out of order . . . (*Breaks off.*)

MARINA. Oh, *no*, Rosina ! Why on earth should anyone want to sneak in like that ?

ROSINA. People do do such things.—I—I suppose they *are* for you ?

MARINA. Who *else* could they be for ?—Oh, perhaps there's a card ! (*Stoops and rummages amongst the roses.*) *Yes*, there *is* !

(Extracts card and begins to read it. As she does so, her expression changes from mild interest to puzzlement and then to a sort of blank incredulity. She sinks rather weakly into the couch, then hurriedly puts the card in her handbag.)

ROSINA *(picking up flowers)*. I'll put them in water.

MARINA *(in sudden agitation)*. Oh, no !

ROSINA *(in surprise)*. Not ?

MARINA. Oh, well—yes, I suppose you'd better.

(ROSINA glances at MARINA in some perplexity and bears flowers out. Exit A. and to L.)

(MARINA immediately fishes card from handbag and reads it again as if unable to believe her eyes. After a moment of dazed thought she throws a scared look at French windows, puts card away again, puts handbag on back of couch, rises, hurries to French windows and looks out right and left. Then, still greatly disturbed, she returns into room and goes over to mirror. Here, for a moment, she appraises her reflection—turning her head this way and that— dabbing at her hair. A smugly pleased look appears on her face and when she moves away to back of couch, there is an excited glint in her eye. She takes a compact from her handbag and begins embellishing her face.

Enter ALBERTO and TOMASSO, L. Both are munching sandwiches.)

ALBERTO *(talking to TOMASSO over his shoulder, does not at first see MARINA)* . . . because I shall be frightfully annoyed, you know, if she's not what you say she is. *(Grins, takes a bite at his sandwich, sees MARINA and stops in his tracks.)*

(TOMASSO comes to a halt behind him. Both stand transfixed, ALBERTO with the sandwich to his mouth.)

MARINA *(looks up and smiles)*. You couldn't wait, then. I'm sorry I was so long. *(Continues with compact.)*

(Both men's eyes simultaneously fall on the blank space on the coffee-table. ALBERTO turns his head sharply and their eyes meet in a startled look. Then they cast rapid glances round the room.)

(*Putting away compact.*) Well, I'll just go and put my things away, and then we can have some lunch. (*Picks up hat.*)

(*Enter* ROSINA (A) *from* L. *Carrying the flowers now in a vase,* ROSINA *comes down to coffee-table, puts them on it and goes straight out again,* L.)

(ALBERTO *and* TOMASSO *stand goggling—both completely at a loss.* MARINA, *for her own reasons, is also acutely constrained. The result is a very awkward silence.*)

(*Indicating flowers.*) Lovely, aren't they ?

(ALBERTO *opens his mouth to reply, thinks better of it and clears his throat.*)

I—er—I just couldn't resist them.

ALBERTO (*throws a puzzled look at* TOMASSO). What did you say ?

MARINA. They stood there looking so beautiful—simply *asking* to be bought.

ALBERTO. Bought ?

MARINA (*mischievously*). Well, if my *hus*band won't buy me flowers—(*Begins to move upstage*)—I must do it myself—(*Tweaks* ALBERTO'S *ear as she passes*)—mustn't I ? (*Glances at* ALBERTO'S *sandwich.*) Don't spoil your lunch, dear ! (*Smiles.*)

(*Exit* MARINA (A) *and to* R.)

ALBERTO (*bewildered*). What's she playing at ?

TOMASSO. Perhaps she thought she *did* buy them.

ALBERTO. Don't be idiotic !

TOMASSO. No, I mean—perhaps she bought another lot which haven't come yet.

ALBERTO. Oh, I see what you . . . (*Breaks off and starts forward in sudden alarm.*) *Wait* a minute ! (*Throws his sandwich on coffee-table and begins searching in the flowers.*)

(*Enter* ROSINA, L.)

ROSINA. Lunch is ready, Signor—when you are.

ALBERTO.   Oh—thank you !

(ROSINA *turns away.*)

Er—Rosina !

(ROSINA *halts and turns enquiringly.*)

(*Off-handedly.*)   Er—was there any sort of—card or anything with these, d'you know ?

ROSINA (*smiling brightly*).   The Signora has it.

ALBERTO (*laughs faintly and falsely*).   Oh—the Signora has it !

ROSINA.   In her handbag !

ALBERTO.   Oh, in her . . . !   Oh, thanks very much !

(*Exit* ROSINA, L.)

She *lied !*

TOMASSO (*unimpressed*).   She did, didn't she ?   (*Sinks into chair,* L.C.).

ALBERTO.   She's got his note and she's got his flowers—and she's *lied* about it.

TOMASSO (*shrugs*).   Well—according to you—(*Takes a bite of sandwich*)—there's a chink in *every* woman's armour.

ALBERTO.   For God's sake don't *eat* when you say things like that !

TOMASSO.   At the moment, presumably, she'll be saying to herself " what sort of a man *is* this ? "

ALBERTO (*anguished*).   You don't *really* think that ?

TOMASSO.   The *curious* stage !   (*Takes a bite of sandwich.*)

ALBERTO.   I can't believe it.   I *won't* believe it !   (*Goes up* R.)

TOMASSO.   Well, I don't know how you're going to disprove it.

ALBERTO.   I shall have to send her *another* lot, that's all.

TOMASSO.   What ?   What for ?

ALBERTO (*coming down* R.)   Well—to see what *hap*pens.   I *must* get it settled *one* way or another.   I can't go on for the rest of my life *not knowing.*

TOMASSO (*changing his tone to one of impatience*).   Don't be an ass, Alberto !   Forget it !

ALBERTO.   How *can* I forget it ?

TOMASSO.   She's em*bar*rassed, that's all.

ALBERTO.   How d'you mean ?

TOMASSO. Well—she doesn't know how to pass it off. It's perfectly natural.

ALBERTO (*getting hopeful—crossing to* TOMASSO). You mean she—just doesn't want to talk about it ?

TOMASSO. That's all !

ALBERTO. Because she feels awkward ?

TOMASSO. Yes.

ALBERTO (*warming to the thought*). Well, I suppose it *is* a bit unpleasant for a woman like Marina, isn't it ?

TOMASSO. Very unpleasant !

ALBERTO. I mean—getting an offensive note like that from some cad she's never heard of ! It's a bit of a *shock*.

TOMASSO. Certainly it is !

ALBERTO. Well, of course ! That's what it is. (*Sits on* L. *arm of couch and begins to laugh with relief*.) Poor old Marina ! I suppose she thought we'd laugh at her.—Well, I suppose the best way to help her out is to ignore the whole thing.

(*Enter* MARINA (A) *from* R. *She is now without her outdoor things.* TOMASSO *continues eating his sandwich.*)

(*Pleasantly.*) Did you get your shoes, dear ?

MARINA (*discontentedly*). No. (*Goes to mirror and dabs at her hair.*)

ALBERTO (*concerned*). Oh !—Hadn't they got what you wanted ?

MARINA. No.

ALBERTO (*sympathetically*). Oh, I'm sorry ! Well, you must try somewhere else.

MARINA (*unenthusiastically*). Oo—I don't think I'll bother.

ALBERTO. But you *must* have pretty things to go away with, darling.

MARINA (*hesitates*). Well—I—I don't know whether I *shall* go, after all. (*Moves to coffee-table.*)

ALBERTO. What ? (*Throws a startled glance at* TOMASSO *and rises.*) Why not ?

(TOMASSO *stops munching and watches apprehensively.*)

MARINA (*not very anxious to meet* ALBERTO'S *eye*). Oh—I don't know ! (*Takes a cigarette.*)

ALBERTO (*suspiciously*). What's made you change your mind ?

MARINA.   Well—(*lights cigarette*)—it *isn't* quite fair on you, I suppose.

ALBERTO.   But you've known that all along.

MARINA.   Well, I've been thinking it over, that's all. (*Wandering over to window,* R.)—And then there's Tina.   She *is* so dull—and her teeth *do* stick out in the most *irritating* way.

ALBERTO.   Now, look here, Marina !   Half-an-hour ago you wanted a holiday to get away from *my* face.   Now you *don't* want a holiday to get away from *Tina's*.   What's the *matter* with you ?

MARINA (*looking absently out of window*).   I thought you'd be pleased.

ALBERTO.   Well, I'm not pleased.   I don't like all this chopping and changing.   I think you're behaving in a very silly way—and I think you *need* a holiday.

MARINA (*turns her head*).   You're not very consistent, you know.   (*Returns her gaze to street.*)

ALBERTO.   And why are you looking out of the window ?

MARINA (*turns in surprise*).   Why shouldn't I look out of the window ?

TOMASSO (*interposing hurriedly*).   I say !   (*Rises.*)

MARINA.   Yes ?

TOMASSO.   She *did* say that lunch was ready, you know.

MARINA (*at once crossing*).   Oh !—Then let's go in.   (*Halts at flowers, considers them, then picks them up and bears them* R.)—I think these 'ud look better here, though—(*places vase on desk in window*)—don't you ?

(*Both men stand speechless.*)

(*Admires the. effect, then turns, hurries across, takes* TOMASSO's *arm and urges him* L.)   Come !—You must be starving.

(TOMASSO, *clutching the remains of his sandwich, throws an anxious backward glance at* ALBERTO *as he is thrust through doorway.*)

(*Exit* TOMASSO, L.)

Come, dear !

(*Exit* MARINA, L.)

(ALBERTO *stands rooted to the spot, staring at vase.*   BERNARDO's *grinning face appears at window, up* R., *and passes on.*

Enter BERNARDO, F.W.)

BERNARDO (*halting furtively in doorway*).   Psst !
ALBERTO (*turns—angrily*).   Go away !
BERNARDO (*his grin disappearing*).   Uh ?
ALBERTO (*loudly*).   *Go away !*

(*Turns and strides*, L.)

CURTAIN

ACT II

SCENE : *The same, mid-afternoon, ten days later.*

(Curtain rises on an empty stage. The roses, now a collection of one or two very overblown blossoms and a number of naked stalks, still stand in window, R. BERNARDO'S whistle is heard (off). After a slight pause his face appears cautiously at window, up R., looks in and moves on.

Enter BERNARDO (F.W.). *He carries a small posy made up of two roses—one white and one red—and a sprig of ivy. He halts warily in the doorway, listens and again emits the whistle. At a slight noise (off) he bobs back outside and is seen to pass the window in haste.*

Exit BERNARDO (F.W.).

Enter MARINA (A) *from* R. *She is dressed informally. Having evidently heard the whistle, she enters slowly, hesitantly, with one hand to her throat and her eyes directed in a sort of horrified fascination towards the open French-windows. She halts just inside the room.*

Enter ROSINA (L.).)

ROSINA (*enters precipitately, makes for* F.W., *sees* MARINA *and comes to an abrupt halt*). Oh !

MARINA. Rosina !

ROSINA. Yes, Signora ?

MARINA. Did you hear anything ?

ROSINA (*trying to look innocent*). Hear anything !

MARINA. Yes, a sort of a—a sort of a whistle—a low, mysterious whistle !

ROSINA (*blankly*). No, Signora !

MARINA. It sounded almost—in here.

ROSINA. In *here !* But, how *could* it be ?

MARINA. It sounded . . . (*indicates* F.W.). Will you look ?

ROSINA (*at once hurrying to* F.W.). Of course, but . . . (*Breaks off, goes out on to terrace, casts a wary look back into the room and makes a small, urgent signal to someone to go away.*)

(MARINA *stands waiting apprehensively.*)

(*Cont. : comes back into room*) Nobody there !

MARINA (*with a note of disappointment*). Oh, dear ! (*Moves wearily down.*) I've heard it several times lately.

ROSINA (*lightly*). It's your imagination, Signora—playing you tricks.

MARINA (*gloomily*). It wouldn't surprise me in the least.

ROSINA (*playfully*). You'll be seeing things next.

MARINA. I know. That's what I'm afraid of. (*Begins to sink into chair,* L.C.)

(*Telephone bell begins to ring.* MARINA *starts violently and jumps to her feet again.*)

ROSINA (*moves swiftly to phone, lifts receiver*). Hullo !—No, this is 0-five-o-seven ! (*Replaces receiver, turns with a smile.*) Somebody wanting the florist !

MARINA. Oh ! (*Relaxing again in mingled relief and disappointment, sits* L.C.)

ROSINA (*regarding her with concern*). Are you all right, Signora ?

MARINA. Yes, I'm . . . (*Breaks off and rises again.*) I—I think I'm a little restless, that's all. (*Moves over to window,* R.)

ROSINA. Nothing worrying you ?

MARINA (*airily*). No—no ! I expect it's just the weather or—something I had for lunch or—something.

ROSINA. But it's *lovely* weather and you didn't *eat* any lunch and, anyway, for *days* now you've been getting more and more . . .

MARINA (*interrupting—her attention electrified by something in the street*). Rosina !

ROSINA. Yes ?

MARINA (*urgently*). Come here !

(ROSINA *runs to window,* R.)

(*Cont. : pointing*) What's that man doing ?

ROSINA. Uh ?

MARINA. There ! On the other side of the street ! What's he doing, just standing there like that, not doing anything ?

ROSINA. It's a *bus* stop.

MARINA (*relaxing again*). Oh, so it is ! (*Turns away, moves to couch.*) I—I *do* seem to be a little nervous, don't I ?

ROSINA (*concerned*). What is it, Signora ?

MARINA (*sits couch—hesitates*). It's so *silly* !

ROSINA (*at once goes to* MARINA, *sits beside her and takes both her hands*). Never mind ! Tell Rosina !

MARINA (*hesitates again*). Well—it's these flowers.

ROSINA. Flowers ! You mean the ones you've been passing on to me every day ?

MARINA. Yes.—Ten days ago, when the first lot came— (*indicates the wreckage in the window*)—I let you think that they were from my mother—and I suppose you've assumed that all the others have been, too.

ROSINA (*half apologetically*). Well I—*hav*en't, really. I—didn't think it seemed *lik*ely.

MARINA. No—well, of course they weren't.

ROSINA. A *man* ?

(*Biting her lip,* MARINA *nods.*)

(*Cont. : a little thrilled*) Someone who—*should*n't ?

(*Turning her head away,* MARINA *nods.*)

(*Cont. : deeply impressed*). Auhh ! (*Slight, thoughtful pause.*)—But if they worry you so much, why don't you just send them back and tell him not to ?

MARINA. I don't know where they *come* from.

ROSINA. You don't know where he *lives* ?

MARINA. I don't know who he *is*.

ROSINA. Mama mia ! (*Releases* MARINA'S *hands and sits back in wonderment.*)

MARINA (*full of self-pity*). All I know is that he's suddenly arrived in the middle of my life with his notes and his roses and—taken possession of me.

ROSINA (*startled*). Signora !

MARINA. If I knew what he looked like, even, it mightn't be so bad—because, if I didn't happen to like his face or something, I could defend myself with the thought of *that*. But, as it is, I've nothing but my own mental conception of him—which is *mar*vellous.

ROSINA (*alarmed*). But you don't mean you can't de*fend* yourself ?

MARINA. What can I *do* ? If he'd been flesh and blood I could have smacked his face and done with it when he started. But this wraith, this shadow, this formless, bodyless *e*ssence of masculinity—keeping *on* like this—it isn't *fair*.

ROSINA. But what does he *want* ?

MARINA. I daren't let myself think.

ROSINA (*comfortingly*). Well, anyway—so long as he re*mains* formless and bodyless, you needn't worry about *that* part of it, need you ?

MARINA. No, but how long is he going to *stop* that way ? (*Gets a little tearful.*)

ROSINA (*compassionately*) Poor Signora ! (*With sudden vehemence.*) *A*ren't they beasts ?

MARINA. Oh, no ! No, you mustn't think that ! There's nothing beastly about him. There couldn't be. He has such lovely thoughts.

ROSINA (*cynically*). Because a man gives you flowers, it doesn't follow that he's got lovely thoughts, you know. (*Glances at* F.W.)

MARINA. Oh, but his letters . . . !

ROSINA. His . . . ! You mean, he's *wr*itten ?

MARINA. Several times ! (*Emotionally.*) And it's *won*-derful !

ROSINA (*rising*). You know—what *you*'ve done is to form a picture of something too good to be *pos*sible—and the sooner you see just an *ord*inary man, the better. (*Moves behind couch.*)

MARINA (*interrupting*). Oh, but he c*ould*n't be *ord*inary. I mean, everything a*bout* him ! Even his *flowers* ! *N*obody delivers them. They just app*ear*. Somebody—*some*body must come right into this room.

ROSINA (*thoughtfully*). Perhaps—what with one thing and another—perhaps we'd better have that catch repaired.

MARINA (*in alarm*). Oh, no, Rosina ! I couldn't bear it if I didn't get my flowers.

(ROSINA *makes a little gesture of despair and looks at* MARINA *as if she doesn't know what to do with her.*)

(*Cont.*) As a matter of fact, I think that's why I'm so fidgety this afternoon—because they haven't come yet.

ROSINA (*moving round couch*). Well, they won't come while there's anybody here, so—you go and lie down for a little while and I'll bring you a nice hot cup of tea. (*Smiles and holds out her hands.*) Will you ?

MARINA (*allows herself to be drawn up*). You're a dear girl, Rosina. (*Smiles wanly and kisses her.*) And you must forgive me but—I've no-one else to comfort me. (*Moving dispiritedly up* L.) Even my husband didn't come home for lunch to-day. (*At archway.*) The *post* hasn't come yet, either.

(*Exit* MARINA (A) *and to* R.)

(ROSINA *moves at once to telephone, lifts receiver, dials.* BERNARDO'S *face appears at window, up* R., *looks in and passes on. Enter* BERNARDO (F.W.). *Still carrying his posy, he sees* ROSINA *and halts on the threshold.*)

ROSINA (*into phone*). Hullo, is that . . . ? Is Signor Bernardo there, please ? (*Waits.*)

BERNARDO (*enjoying the situation, laughs silently, then——*) Pssst !

ROSINA (*turns with a start*). Oh !

BERNARDO (*highly gratified*). Did you want me ?

ROSINA (*grimly*). Yes, I did ! (*Replaces receiver and goes to him.*) Now, look here ! (*Wagging a finger at him.*) I know perfectly well you've been bringing flowers into this house !

(BERNARDO *puts on an innocent expression and opens his mouth to reply, but gets no chance.*)

(*Cont.*) And it's not a *bit* of good denying it, because I know your methods.

BERNARDO (*smirks with self-satisfaction*). Which are unique !

ROSINA. Well, let's hope so.—But what I want to know is—who's sending them ?

BERNARDO (*his smile disappearing*). What ?

ROSINA. Who do they *come* from ?

BERNARDO (*unable to believe his ears*). You're asking *me*—Bernardo—to betray my sacred, professional trust ?

ROSINA. I'm asking you to . . .

BERNARDO (*interrupting in high indignation*). If I were a *doc*tor, would you expect me to divulge the secrets of my consulting room ?

ROSINA (*impatiently*). Oh, don't talk such . . .

BERNARDO (*interrupting*). Or a father-confessor ! If I were a fa . . .

ROSINA (*interrupting*). Well, you're *not* a father-confessor or anything *like* one—and Signora Verani's being driven out of her *mind*.

BERNARDO (*with dignity*). What has Signora Verani to do with it ?

ROSINA. Well, she's getting the flowers, isn't she ?

BERNARDO. You'll forgive me for saying so, but Signora Verani cannot be getting any flowers which *I* deliver. (*Sits on* R. *arm of couch*.)

ROSINA. Why not ?

BERNARDO. Because they happen to be for *S*ignor Verani.

ROSINA. Uh ?

BERNARDO. And *he* wants them for a certain ripe young Countess in the Via Guittone d'Arezzo.

ROSINA (*staggered*). He wants them for a . . . ! You mean he's . . . ? (*Breaks off*.)

BERNARDO. Certainly ! Why shouldn't he ?

ROSINA. How do *you* know, anyway ?

BERNARDO (*loftily*). I happen to have his confidence.

ROSINA. He *told* you ?

BERNARDO. He told me when he *sta*rted. He naturally hasn't troubled to mention it again every day since. There's no need. He knows I'm sensitive to these things.

ROSINA. *Well !*

BERNARDO. But I hand them to him personally—so there must be somebody *else* bringing the flowers which your Signora gets.

ROSINA. But who could it *be ?*

BERNARDO (*rising*). What are they ? Perhaps I can recognise the technique.

ROSINA. Red roses ! Two dozen a day !

BERNARDO (*with a sneer*). Huh ! That doesn't help much. (*Moves away* L.)

ROSINA. There can't be many people who do that.

BERNARDO (*scornfully*). They *all* do it—all the beginners—that's what the *C*ountess is getting, *too*.

ROSINA (*amazed*). Red roses ? Two dozen a day ?

BERNARDO. Yes.

ROSINA. But how extraordinary !

BERNARDO (*in a superior way*). Not at all ! It's the mark of the amateur, that's all. They *always* go for red roses. The only extraordinary thing about it is the stupidity of the method.

ROSINA. Huh ?

BERNARDO (*becoming expansive—returns to her*). Not that I've anything a*gainst* red roses, mind you, *as such.* (*Holds up his posy and demonstrates.*) A single bloom with its simple message—what could be more charming ?—Add a white one, and you begin to get something ! Red for the lover—white for the innocent beloved—in unity. (*Pauses and glances at her.*)

(ROSINA, *not displeased, hangs her head shyly.*)

(*Cont.*) Entwine it with a sprig of ivy, and you have a poem. (*Gesticulating in sudden anger, strides off round couch.*) But *bun*ches of red roses *every* day ! It's like a cracked gramophone record—" I love you, I love you, I love you, I love you, I love you ! "

(ROSINA *laughs.*)

(*Cont. : returning to* ROSINA) I don't *won*der the Signora's being driven out of her mind. (*Smiles charmingly, proffers posy.*) For *you*, Rosina ! (*Makes a little bow.*)

ROSINA (*taking posy with a little curtsy*). Thank you, Bernardo !

BERNARDO (*suddenly thoughtful*). What does she *do* with them all ?

ROSINA. Well, she can't dis*play* them, so she has to give them to *me* to get rid of.—My bedroom's simply *stuffed* with them.

BERNARDO (*slyly*). Perhaps we could do a deal.

ROSINA. You mean . . . ? (*Breaks off.*)

BERNARDO. Why not ? I have a *mar*ket for red roses. Maybe I could make a little profit for us both.

ROSINA (*thinks rapidly*). Come back later and I'll bring you down a couple of armfuls.

BERNARDO. Good !

ROSINA. You must go now ! I've got to get her some tea. (*Holds up her face to be kissed.*)

(BERNARDO *kisses her lustily and turns for* F.W.)

(*Cont.*) (*Turns away* L., *looks at posy, halts*).   I say !
    BERNARDO.   Yes ?   (*Returns to her eagerly.*)
    ROSINA (*suspiciously—indicating posy*).   You didn't say what
the *ivy* meant.
    BERNARDO (*grinning doubtfully*).   Oh—that was just for my
own satisfaction, really.
    ROSINA.   Well, I'd like to know, if you don't mind.

(BERNARDO *hesitates, grinning wickedly, then whispers in her ear.*)

(*Cont.—outraged—pushes him away*).   Oh !—Well, you can *keep*
your·beastly poem !   (*Throws posy at his head.*)
    BERNARDO (*ducks, laughs, skips to* F.W. *and turns*).   That's
nothing !—Wait till I bring you an orchid in a bed of lotus
leaves !

(*Exit* BERNARDO (F.W.).)

(ROSINA *glares after him, turns away* L., *remembers posy, returns for*
it, picks it up, regards it and smiles gently despite herself.

Front door bell rings, off.

Not knowing what to do with the posy, ROSINA *hesitates, flustered.*
Finally she conceals it beneath her apron and starts towards
archway to answer bell.

Enter MARINA (A) *from* R.   *She rushes across archway.*

Exit MARINA (A) *to* L.

ROSINA *changes her direction and goes off* L.

Exit ROSINA (L).

There is a pause and voices are heard (*off*).   *Enter* MARINA *and*
ALBERTO (A) *from* L.   ALBERTO *wears a lounge suit.*)

    MARINA.   Why didn't you come up the side way, then ?
    ALBERTO.   Because I was at the front door before I discovered
I'd left my key behind.

MARINA (*complainingly*). I thought it was the post.

ALBERTO (*bitterly*). Well I'm sorry to disappoint you, but it wasn't, it was only your husband. (*Halting in surprise, suddenly realising what she has said.*) What do you mean you thought it was the post? Hasn't it come yet?

MARINA. No.

ALBERTO. But it's—(*glances at his wrist-watch*)—nearly an hour late.

MARINA. I know. (*Trying to be off-hand.*) Perhaps it's—not coming to-day.

ALBERTO. Oh, it's coming, all right. (*Moves R.*)

MARINA. How do you know? Are you expecting a letter?

ALBERTO. No. (*Halts and looks at her keenly.*) Are you?

MARINA. No.

ALBERTO (*continuing to bookcase*). What's all the fuss about, then? (*Takes out a novel, moves to couch and sits.*)

MARINA (*watching in dismay, casts an anxious glance at F.W.*). Are you *staying*?

ALBERTO. What d'you mean " *stay*ing " ? I *live* here. (*Opens book.*)

MARINA. But it's not your usual time.

ALBERTO. Well, I thought I'd get finished at the office and have a nice, quiet afternoon at home. (*Settles himself.*)

MARINA (*increasingly worried*). You mean you're going to sit there and read for the rest of the *day?*

ALBERTO. D'you mind?

MARINA. No, *I* don't mind, only—I wish you'd let us *know* when you're going to do these things.

ALBERTO. Do I have to make arrangements in ad*vance* every time I walk into my own house?

MARINA. Of *course* not, but . . .

ALBERTO (*interrupting*). Perhaps you'd like me to fill in a *form* every morning.

MARINA. It throws things out, that's all. (*Sits arm of chair, L.C.*)

ALBERTO (*eyeing her narrowly*). Why—what were you doing?

MARINA. Lying down !

ALBERTO. Then go and *lie* down ! *I* shan't disturb you.

MARINA. You *have* disturbed me.

ALBERTO. Oh, for pity's sake ! (*Turns ill-humouredly to book.*)

(Pause.)

MARINA *(slides into chair, stares at him and fidgets—then, conversationally.)* Much traffic on the roads ?   *(She is determined not to let him settle.)*

ALBERTO *(looking up perplexed).*   Eh ?

MARINA.   It was simply *aw*ful yesterday.   Bus after bus after bus after bus !

(ALBERTO *looks at her in a rather bewildered way and goes back to his book.)*

(Cont. : after slight pause) And the *taxi*-cabs, my dear !   You should have *seen* them !   *Cab* after . . .

ALBERTO *(interposing irritably)* . . . *cab* after *cab* after *cab !* If you *want* to sit and chat, just say so and I'll . . .   *(Breaks off, closing book.)*

MARINA *(rising).*   *I* don't want to sit and chat.

ALBERTO.   All *right* then !   *(Opens book again.)*

MARINA *(wandering away to window R.).*   But there *was* a time when you used to en*joy* a little intelligent conversation.

ALBERTO.   D'you call *that* intelligent conversation—" bus after bus ? "   *(Returns to book but shows that he is uneasily conscious of MARINA'S restlessness.)*

(Pause—looking idly out of the window, MARINA begins humming.)

MARINA.   What *is* the time ?

ALBERTO *(looks at wrist-watch).*   Three-thirty !—Why ?

MARINA.   Nothing !—It seems to drag so, that's all.

ALBERTO *(wearily).*   Why *don't* you go and lie down ?   *(Continues reading.)*

(Pause.   MARINA hums a few more bars.)

MARINA *(sadly).*   It's such a lovely day !

(No response from ALBERTO.   Slight pause.)

(Cont. : with sudden severity) I should have thought a man of your age would be only too glad to get out in it.

ALBERTO (*warily*).   How d'you mean ?

MARINA.   Well, do something *vigorous*—play *tennis* or something !

ALBERTO.   .Oh !—would you ?

MARINA.   You'll be getting fat if you sit about the place like that.

ALBERTO.   Now, look here ! If I *want* to sit and enjoy myself with a good book in my own house, I'm damn well *going* to. (*Goes back to book.*)

MARINA (*moving down to coffee-table*).   You don't even seem to be enjoying it. (*Takes a cigarette.*) May I have a light, please ?

(ALBERTO *laboriously lays down book, picks up matches and holds them out to her, but she waits for him to strike one for her. This he does with an ill grace. She lights cigarette.*)

(*Cont.*) Thank you !

(ALBERTO *takes up book.* MARINA *steps over his legs wanders to radio and switches it on. A loud and strident march blares forth.* ALBERTO *lays down book with an air of frustrated exasperation.* MARINA *turns away and leans on the back of chair* L.C., *apparently listening attentively.* ALBERTO *folds his arms and leans back in ironical resignation.*

Pause.*)

ALBERTO (*loudly, to top the music*).   Marina !
MARINA (*loudly*).   Yes ?
ALBERTO.   Do you like that ?
MARINA.   No.

(ALBERTO *picks up book, rises and stalks up to bookcase—his step unconsciously falling into time with the music.* MARINA *watches hopefully.* ALBERTO *puts away book and, again taking the rhythm of the march, strides across to her.*)

ALBERTO.   Then why do you turn it on ?
MARINA.   It's better than nothing, don't you think ?
ALBERTO.   No, I do *not* think it's better than nothing.
MARINA (*mildly*).   Switch it off, then ! (*Moves down* c.)

(ALBERTO *turns to radio, switches it off and remains for a moment facing the wall as if fighting his emotions.* MARINA *picks up a magazine and seats herself with it in* ALBERTO'S *place on couch.*)

ALBERTO (*turns—in a controlled voice*).   Marina!

MARINA (*without looking up*).   Um?

ALBERTO.   What's happened to us?

MARINA (*looking up—surprised*).   Happened?

ALBERTO.   Yes—what's the matter?

MARINA.   Matter?

ALBERTO (*controls himself with an effort*).   Look!   Don't keep on repeating everything I say—there's a good girl—it annoys me.

MARINA.   But I don't know what . . .

ALBERTO.   And *don't* pretend you don't know what I'm *talk*ing about because I'm trying *very* hard to keep my *tem*per.

MARINA.   If it'll improve your temper, I'll be glad to admit anything, dear.   (*Goes back to magazine.*)

ALBERTO.   Don't drive me too far, Marina!   We're still on speaking terms.   For heaven's sake let's keep *that* much.   (*Comes down to behind couch—in a changed tone.*)   Why do we bicker like this?   Why do we behave in this childish and unpleasant way?

MARINA (*without looking up—sweetly reasonable*).   You should speak for yourself, Alberto dear!

ALBERTO (*angrily*).   If I ad*mit* to a share in the blame, my girl, it's merely because I want to be *fair*.

MARINA.   And you don't really mean it?

ALBERTO.   No!

MARINA.   So it's all *my* fault!

ALBERTO.   Well, look at this afternoon, for instance!—Why do you do everything you can think of to annoy me?

MARINA.   What makes you think I'm doing everything I can think of?

ALBERTO.   You see?   You can't even answer a civil question like *that!*   (*Turns away* L. *in despair.*)

(MARINA, *her legs crossed, begins nervously to swing the upper one.*)

(*Cont.: turning back to her, with a note of pleading*).   Marina—I *know* you're unhappy.   I know so well what you *look* like when you're unhappy.

MARINA (*tartly*).   You should do—by now!

ALBERTO (*with iron control*).   I'm not going to get angry—

because I know that—in some way you're—suffering—and, believe me it—distresses me beyond all measure—to see you suffer. (*Suddenly shouting in fury.*) And don't swing your *leg* like that when I'm talking to you ! (*Turns away fuming.*)

(MARINA *looks up in faintly pained surprise, uncrosses her legs, shifts her position and continues with magazine.*)

(*Cont. : with his back turned*). I'm sorry, I'm not myself !

MARINA (*unkindly*). Well—that's a step in the right direction, anyway.

ALBERTO (*turns and regards her with anguish, then comes impulsively round couch and sits beside her—imploringly*). Marina—can't I help ?

(MARINA *does not reply, but sits staring at magazine. She turns a page.*)

(*Cont.*) Can't you tell me ?—*I*'ll understand, whatever it is. I *pro*mise I will.

(MARINA *turns a page.*)

Or would it be better to—to try and for*get* it—whatever it is that—seems to have come between us ?

(MARINA *turns a page.*)

(*Cont.*) Marina !—Can't we start again—while there's still time ?

(MARINA *does not reply, but she lowers her magazine and is evidently listening.*)

(*Cont. : encouraged*) Look ! Let's go away for a bit. Let's try that.—The sea !—Ostia !—It's lovely there now.—Deserted and peaceful ! We could *be* there in time to see the sun go down.—Do you remember the sunsets at Viareggio, Marina ?

(MARINA, *with bent head, nods.*)

Then, let's do it—*now !*—Chuck a few things into a bag and get the car out and . . . (*Breaks off as——*)

(*Front door bell rings* (*off*). *Both sit up electrified.*)

MARINA (*trying not to appear too eager*). Oh!—(*Rising.*) Excuse me a minute! (*Walks nonchalantly up to archway, then suddenly breaks into a run.*)

(*Exit* MARINA (A) *and to* L.)

(ALBERTO *sits for a moment looking wretchedly defeated, then he rises, wanders aimlessly up to* F.W. *and stands with his back turned, dejectedly looking out. He turns his head as* MARINA'S *voice is heard, off.*)

(*Off—complainingly*) I can't think what's happened to it.

(*Enter* MARINA *and* TOMASSO (A) *from* L. TOMASSO *wears a lounge-suit.*)

TOMASSO (*as they enter*). They're very erratic nowadays.
ALBERTO (*without enthusiasm*). Oh, it's you! (*Turns away again.*)
TOMASSO (*amused*). Yes—she thought it was the post. (*Sensing trouble, his smile dies and he glances from one to the other.*)

(ALBERTO *remains with his back turned. There is an uncertain pause.*)

MARINA (*with sudden brightness*). Well, how *are* you, Tomasso dear?
TOMASSO. Oh, I'm all right, thanks! How are you?
MARINA. Oh, I'm *very* well!
TOMASSO. *That's* good!

(*Silence.*)

MARINA. Well, I—er—I expect you two want to chat, so I'll just . . . (*Trails off and begins to back towards archway.*)
TOMASSO (*slightly surprised*). *I* don't want to chat—(*to* ALBERTO)—do *you*?
ALBERTO. Who, *me*? Chat? Last thing I want to do.
TOMASSO (*to* MARINA). I came in to pick you up.

MARINA (*blankly*). Pick *me* up ?

ALBERTO (*bitterly*). That's the latest thing—repeating everything you say.

TOMASSO (*to* MARINA). We were going to the flower-show.

MARINA. Oh, *were* we, dear ? I'm *so* sorry !

TOMASSO. Did you forget ?

MARINA (*evasively*). Well—*any*way, I'm afraid I'm not quite up to it.

TOMASSO. Oh, I'm sorry !

MARINA. I was just going to lie down.—D'you mind very much ?

TOMASSO. Of course not ! I'm not all that keen on flowers.

MARINA (*at archway*). No—they *are* things you have to be in the mood for, aren't they ?

(*Exit* MARINA (A) *and to* R.)

(ALBERTO *at once comes to life and moves to telephone.*)

TOMASSO (*indicating archway*). What's up ?

ALBERTO (*lifting receiver, dialling*). Oh, we're in a *fright*ful mess.

TOMASSO (*going to him—in alarm*). Why, what's happened ?

ALBERTO. She's going all to pieces. I'm *terr*ibly worried about her. I don't know *what* to . . . (*into phone.*) Hullo ! Bernardo ?—All right, you can bring 'em up now ! (*Hangs up and turns.*) I simply don't know what . . .

TOMASSO (*interrupting angrily*). Do you mean to tell me that you're *still* going on with this preposterous performance ?

ALBERTO (*with a note of terror*). Tomasso—I *can't stop !*

TOMASSO. Huh ?

ALBERTO (*seizes vase of bare and drooping stems*). See these ?—They're the original lot. She won't let anybody *touch* 'em. Says she *likes* 'em mature.—Look at 'em !—M*ature !* (*Replaces vase.*)—Well, the next day, as you know, I sent her some more. (*Begins pacing restlessly.*)

TOMASSO (*sourly*). I expressed myself about that at the time.

ALBERTO. But I couldn't credit my *sen*ses. I *had* to have confirmation.

TOMASSO. And you got it ?

ALBERTO. Yes.

TOMASSO (*moving away* L.). Serves you damn well right !

ALBERTO (*pleadingly*). Tomasso, do try to be a bit sympathetic about this, old boy. I'm having a *hell* of a time.

TOMASSO (*wearily—sitting* L.C.). All right! What happened then?

ALBERTO. Well, I had to give her a chance, hadn't I? (*Comes to a halt behind couch.*) I mean, you've got to be just. You can't condemn a woman on the strength of that. I had to give her better nature *time* to work. It was only *fair*.

TOMASSO So you went on sending roses?

ALBERTO (*trying not to look shamefaced*). Yes. (*Recommences pacing.*)

TOMASSO. And it didn't function?

ALBERTO. What didn't?

TOMASSO. Her better nature.

ALBERTO. It didn't be*gin* to. (*Resentfully.*) I don't know what's the *matter* with the damn thing.

TOMASSO. Well, what happened then?

ALBERTO. Then I thought I'd lay off—so, on the sixth day, I stopped it.

TOMASSO. You did?

ALBERTO. Yes—and she nearly went crazy. Wouldn't eat! Couldn't sleep! Couldn't sit still for two minutes at a time! Just wandered about the place looking like something out of Milton's " Paradise Lost "!—So, on the seventh day—I started up again.

(TOMASSO *groans.*)

What *else* could I do? I couldn't stand by and see the poor soul suffering like that. It was breaking my heart.

TOMASSO. Look! If you're trying to sell me the idea that this abominable persecution is really an *act* of *grace* on your part, I tell you straight, you're . . .

ALBERTO (*interrupting—coming to a halt down* L.) D'you think it's any *ple*asure to me to hear her burst into song the moment she gets a bunch of flowers from another man?

TOMASSO (*startled*). What other man?

ALBERTO. This *my*stery fool! *Me!*

TOMASSO. Oh!

ALBERTO. But I can't let the woman go *mad* before my *eyes*, can I?—Look at her this afternoon! Half out of her mind because her roses are an hour or so late and the post hasn't come!

TOMASSO. What's the post got to do with it ?

ALBERTO. Oh, didn't I tell you ? (*Quite resentfully.*) He's been *writing* her !

TOMASSO (*starting to rise—portentously*). Do you mean to tell me . . . ? (*Breaks off and checks his rise as——*)

(*Front door bell rings, off.*)

ALBERTO. Perhaps that's it, now ! (*Hurries off.*)

(*Exit* ALBERTO (A) *and to* L.)

(TOMASSO *sinks back into his chair. Enter* MARINA (A) *from* R. *She rushes across archway.*)

(*Exit* MARINA (A) *to* L.)

(TOMASSO *gets hurriedly to his feet and stares after her.* BERNARDO'S *face appears at window, up* R, *looks in and passes on. Enter* BERNARDO (F.W.). *He carries a large bunch of red roses.*)

BERNARDO (*halting in doorway*). Psst !

(TOMASSO *starts and turns.*)

(*Entering furtively*) *You* can take these, can't you ? (*Thrusts flowers into* TOMASSO'S *hands and leers.*) I know you're in on it. (*Retreats to* F.W.)—And don't forget, Signor ! Any time *you* want anything ! Any time !

(*Exit* BERNARDO, F.W.)

(TOMASSO *looks at flowers, looks at archway, and panic seizes him. He casts wildly round for somewhere to hide them.*

Enter ROSINA (L.). *She carries a tray of tea-things. She makes for archway, sees* TOMASSO *guiltily trying to conceal the flowers behind the flap of his jacket, and stops in her tracks. Her expression, as she looks at him, changes from amazement to disgust.*)

ROSINA (*advances to him and holds out tray—contemptuously*). All right !—Put 'em on the tray !

(TOMASSO, *at a loss, does so.* ROSINA, *with a look of scorn, bears them towards archway.*)

TOMASSO (*following agitatedly*). But, just a minute . . . !
ROSINA (*interrupting disgustedly*). Well !
TOMASSO. But . . .

(*Exit* ROSINA (A) *and to* R.)

TOMASSO (*moving away* R.). Oh, dear ! (*Looking rather shaken, takes out his pills and swallows a couple. Enter* ALBERTO *and* MARINA (A) *from* L. *They come in silently and glumly.*)
ALBERTO (*to* TOMASSO). Chap trying to sell refrigerators. (*Throws himself into chair,* L.C.)
MARINA (*moving down* C.—*doubtfully thoughtful*). I suppose he *was* trying to sell refrigerators !
ALBERTO. How d'you mean ?
MARINA. Well, there was nothing about him to suggest that he was.
ALBERTO. You wouldn't expect him to have one *with* him, would you ?
MARINA. No, but . . . (*Breaks off.*)
ALBERTO. Why should he say he was, if he wasn't ?
MARINA (*trying not to look self-conscious*). They *do* that, you know—burglars and—people—when they want to find out whether there's a—man in the house.

(ALBERTO *catches* TOMASSO'S *eye and shrugs hopelessly. Enter* ROSINA (A) *from* R.)

ROSINA. I've taken some tea up to your room, Signora.
MARINA (*without much interest*). Oh, thank you, Rosina !

(ROSINA *catches* MARINA'S *eye and makes meaning signals in the direction of the bedroom.*)

(*Catching on*) Oh ! (*Scurries out.*)

(*Exit* MARINA (A) *and to* R.)

(ROSINA *proceeds down to door,* L., *pauses long enough to throw* TOMASSO *a look of intense distaste, and goes out.*)

Exit ROSINA, L.)

ALBERTO (*in surprise*). Why the dirty look ?

TOMASSO (*uncomfortably*). Well—as a matter of fact—I think she may have the idea that—*I*'m the one who's been—— (*Hesitates.*)

ALBERTO (*interposing—incredulously*). Sending the flowers ?

TOMASSO. Yes.

ALBERTO. Nonsense, my dear fellow ! Who could possibly suspect *you* of a thing like that ?

TOMASSO. Well, you see . . .

(MARINA'S *voice is heard, off, uplifted in song.*)

ALBERTO (*sits up*). Listen !

TOMASSO (*moving to couch*). Yes—they've come.—I took 'em in. (*Sits.*)

ALBERTO. Oh !

(*They listen a moment.*)

(*Bitterly*) Huh ! Tosti to-day ! It's always either him or Denza or Tirindelli or some other slushy sentimentalist.

TOMASSO (*taking out a pencil and note-book*). Nice voice, you know ! (*Begins doing sums.*)

ALBERTO. I wish she'd shut up though. I can't think while she's . . .

TOMASSO (*interrupting*). What does she *do* with them all ?

ALBERTO. The roses ? I don't know. I suppose she . . . (*Breaks off suspiciously*). What are *you* doing ?

TOMASSO. Just a minute ! (*Scribbling and muttering.*) That's —five—two . . . Do you realise that at two hundred lire a bloom, you're spending money at the rate of one million, seven hundred and fifty-two thousand lire a year ?

ALBERTO. Well—if you want to know—they're two hundred and fifty lire a bloom.

(*The singing ceases.*)

TOMASSO. Oh, well then . . . ! (*Begins more sums.*)

ALBERTO. Hullo !—She's stopped !—(*Bitterly*.) That'll mean she's sitting down to write and *thank* him now.

TOMASSO (*stops writing*). How can she write and thank him? She doesn't even know where he lives.

ALBERTO (*a little guiltily*). No, but she knows where to write to.

TOMASSO. How?

ALBERTO. He's given her a box-number.

TOMASSO. He's given her a . . . ?

ALBERTO (*interposing*). Yes.

TOMASSO (*incredulously*). And she *writes* him?

ALBERTO (*gloomily*). About ten pages a day.

TOMASSO. Marina answers letters from a—from a lout like that.

ALBERTO. Oh, they're not bad letters, mind you—in their way.

TOMASSO. Oh, they're not!

ALBERTO. Oh, no. I can do that sort of thing as well as the next man, if I want to.

TOMASSO. I see! (*Puts away notebook, etc., and rises—angrily.*) So you trap your wife into a private correspondence with another man so that you can read her *letters*?

ALBERTO (*a little shamefaced*). Why shouldn't I? They're *written* to me.

TOMASSO. They're *not* written to you. They're written to this mystery idiot.—You ought to be ashamed of yourself. (*Turns away and goes to window, R.*)

(ALBERTO *has the grace to look ashamed.*)

After slight pause—turning). What does she *say* to him, anyway?

ALBERTO (*glumly*). Oh, she talks about her poor, bruised soul and all that sort of thing.

TOMASSO. For ten pages?

ALBERTO. It's wonderful what she can do on the subject of her soul. I never realised there was so much to it.—What with it's ideals, aspirations, need for escape and everything!

TOMASSO. Escape from what?

ALBERTO. " Mediocre reality " I think she calls it.—(*Bitterly.*) That's *me*, of course!

TOMASSO. And what do *you* talk about?

ALBERTO (*drearily*). Same sort of thing.

TOMASSO. Your poor soul?

ALBERTO. It's the only common ground we've got.—I *did* try to make a bit of a change the other day.

TOMASSO. Oh?

ALBERTO. Invited her to tell me about her husband.

TOMASSO. And did she?

ALBERTO (*gloomily*). She did.

TOMASSO. And what . . . ?

ALBERTO (*interrupting pathetically*). Don't ask me—there's a good fellow!

TOMASSO (*going up to* F.W.). Well, if you ask *me*—any man who spends hours a day writing about his soul—in block letters—deserves all he gets.

ALBERTO (*sullenly*). I *don't* write in block letters. I use a typewriter.

TOMASSO (*returning to desk*). I don't care if you use a *dup*licating machine. I still think you've done a stupid and disgraceful thing.

ALBERTO (*sulkily*). D'you think I don't realise that?

TOMASSO. I'm glad it's beginning to percolate. (*Sits at desk.*)

ALBERTO (*wretchedly*). She hates me now.

TOMASSO. Nonsense! You've got the poor thing confused, that's all.

ALBERTO. She's simply crazy about this other chap.

TOMASSO. I can't see that that matters—if it's you anyway.

ALBERTO (*rising*). Of *course* it matters. If it were anybody *else* breaking up my home, I could shoot him or something—but it *isn't*, it's *me*. I'm doing it my*self!* (*Begins to stride about.*)

TOMASSO. Then *stop* it, you fool!

ALBERTO (*gesticulating*). I *can't* stop it. I've created this—this monster, and lost control of him. It's like a sort of *Frank*enstein.

TOMASSO. All right! Let it go on for a bit! After all, she's bound to get sick of a chap who does nothing but send roses and typescript.

ALBERTO (*goes to him*). Tomasso, it *can't* go on. Our constitutions won't *stand* it. The place is a *battle*field.

TOMASSO. There's no *need* to fight. Ignore it!

ALBERTO. I *can't* ignore it when I find her lying here motionless with her eyes closed and a silly smile on her face, can I? No decent man would stand for that. I *have* to bring her to. And then what happens? The dream's shattered and in its place is—mediocre reality—*me!* So there's a row. It's inevitable. We insult each other in every way we can think of and immediately rush off to our rooms and write *love*-letters to each other.—It's an intolerable state of affairs. (*Turns away and sits on back of couch with back to audience.*)

(*Enter* MARINA (A) *from* R. *She is humming to herself, and carries the tray of tea-things. She makes for door,* L.)

(*To* MARINA, *glumly.*) Feeling better?
MARINA. *Much* better! I've had such a lovely cup of tea.

(*Smiles and continues out* L., *singing blithely.*)

ALBERTO. You see? (*Gets off back of couch.*) It *can't* go on.
TOMASSO (*rises, walks thoughtfully to chair down* R. *and sits*). What about suicide?
ALBERTO (*pathetically*). Yes, I've thought of that but—who's going to support her when I'm gone? (*Sits* R. *arm of couch.*)
TOMASSO. I don't mean *you*—I mean *him*.
ALBERTO (*bitterly*). Oh, *he* wouldn't commit suicide. He's not the type.—Besides, why should he? He's got everything his own way.
TOMASSO. Well, then, let him get run over by a tram, or something.
ALBERTO. I've thought of that too, but—who's going to *tell* her?
TOMASSO. He needn't be killed outright. There's no reason why he shouldn't suffer for a bit. He can write her from hospital and say he's dying.
ALBERTO. And d'you know what she'd do then?
TOMASSO. What?
ALBERTO. Cherish his memory for the rest of her life.—You don't know that woman.
TOMASSO (*thoughtfully*). Hum!
ALBERTO (*looks at his watch and rises*). Oh, good Lord, it's a quarter past four!—I wish that damn post would come.
TOMASSO. Is she due for a letter?
ALBERTO (*looking rather self-conscious*). Yes—rather an important one! (*Struck by a thought.*) I wonder whether it could have gone under the hatstand! It *did* happen once before. (*Starts for archway.*) I think I'll just . . . (*Breaks off and halts as——*)

(*Enter* MARINA (A) *from* L. *She carries a letter. Hurrying across archway, she disappears* R., *immediately to re-appear round corner.*)

MARINA (*trying to conceal her excitement*). Oh—the post *has* come, dear.

ALBERTO. Has it ?

MARINA. Yes. (*Indicates letter with a little laugh.*) Under the hatstand !

ALBERTO. Oh !

MARINA (*laughing*). Yes, I suddenly remembered. It happened once before.

ALBERTO (*indicating the letter*). For you ?

MARINA (*off-handedly*). Yes, just some—typewritten thing— that's all. Nothing for *you*, my pet.

(*Exit* MARINA (A) *to* R.)

(ALBERTO *goes to cabinet, pours a drink, takes a gulp, spills it down his front, mops himself with a handkerchief, comes down to coffee-table looking very strained, takes a cigarette, lights it with shaking fingers, spilling the matches, throws cigarette into ashtray and tries to put match in his mouth, retrieves cigarette and sinks into couch.* TOMASSO *watches in growing concern.*)

TOMASSO. Are you all right ?

ALBERTO (*under great stress*). Tomasso—this is it !

TOMASSO. Which is what ?

ALBERTO (*indicates archway*). That letter ! It's the *fi*nal test.

TOMASSO (*irascibly*). *Now* what have you been . . . ?

ALBERTO (*holding up a hand*). No, no ! Be gentle with me. I'm at the cross-roads.

TOMASSO (*looks at him with an air of defeat, then rises*). Look ! I think I'll go home, if you don't mind. I shall have flatulence for a week as it is. (*Begins to move upstage.*)

ALBERTO (*rising and going to* TOMASSO). Tomasso, I've . . . (*Breaks off.*)

TOMASSO (*halting*). You've what ?

ALBERTO. He's asked her to meet him.

TOMASSO. What ?

ALBERTO. At the Arch of Settimius in the Foro Romano—at half-past four !

Tomasso.   To-day ?
Alberto.   Yes.

(Tomasso *rapidly looks at his watch.*)

She can just make it.

Tomasso.   But he won't be *there*.   You idiot !
Alberto.   I know.
Tomasso.   Then what are you *play*ing at ?
Alberto.   I felt I had to know—once and for all—how far
she'd go with him.
Tomasso.   Dammit, she *can*'t be un*faith*ful with him.   Even
your sense of the morbid couldn't achieve that.
Alberto.   But if she *goes*, Tomasso . . . (*Breaks off as——*)

(*Enter* Rosina, L.   *Still wearing a haughty look, she makes for
archway.*

Telephone bell begins to ring. Alberto *starts and clutches*
Tomasso.

Rosina *changes direction, goes to phone and lifts receiver.*)

Rosina (*into phone*).   Hullo ?—Yes !—Will you hold on a
minute, please ?   I'll ask her.   (*Puts down receiver and hurries* L.)
Alberto (*turns his head sharply at* Rosina's *final words*).
Who's that ?
Rosina (*coldly*).   A lady !
Alberto (*relaxing*).   Oh !

(*Exit* Rosina (A) *and to* R.)

(*Quite hysterically*) You *see* ?   I'm going *mad !*   For the moment,
I thought it might be *he*.   (*Moves restlessly away.*)   And if he
seems as real as that to *me*—what must he be to *her* ?
Tomasso (*moving away* L.).   I don't care *how* real he seems—
she can't go any further with him than she's gone.
Alberto.   Receiving roses and writing letters is one thing—
but meeting people at the Arch of Settimius is another—because
that's no longer theoretical—that's *practical*.—And if she goes,
Tomasso, I shall know that she's perfectly ready to be unfaithful
to me.   I shall know that—in her heart—she already *is*.

TOMASSO (*looks at his watch*). Well, she'll have to get a move on, if she's going.

ALBERTO. Don't *talk* like that, *please!* (*Hesitates, then moves after* TOMASSO.) I—er—I suppose it's no good asking you to go and stand there for a bit ?

TOMASSO. Where ?

ALBERTO. At the Arch of . . .

TOMASSO (*interrupting*). What for ?

ALBERTO (*a little sheepishly*). Well—just to make sure that that's where she goes—if she *does* go out.

TOMASSO (*walks close up to him*). Alberto—I'd do many things for you—(*angrily*)—but hanging about to try and catch your wife committing mental infidelity is not one of them.

ALBERTO. No, I thought not. (*Sits* L.C.)

(*Enter* ROSINA (A) *from* R. *She crosses to phone and picks up receiver.*)

ROSINA (*into phone*). Hullo !—She's very sorry, Signora, but she won't be able to meet you this afternoon. She has a bad headache and she's going to bed.

ALBERTO (*sitting up*). Uh ?

ROSINA (*into phone*). Yes.—Thank you, Signora ! Good-bye. (*Hangs up.*)

ALBERTO (*rising—excitedly*). Going to bed ?

ROSINA (*crossing—coldly*). She's not very well, Signor.

ALBERTO. Oh, thank God !

(ROSINA *throws him a look of perplexity and goes out* L.)

(*Going to* TOMASSO—*delightedly*) It's all *right*, then !

TOMASSO. Well, of *course* it is.

(*Together they begin to move down* R.)

ALBERTO. I *knew* it couldn't be anything, really.

TOMASSO. Nothing more than a—than an utterly innocent . . .

ALBERTO (*interposing*) . . . romantic disturbance, that's all.

TOMASSO. Exactly !

ALBERTO. She's sound as a bell, my dear fellow.

TOMASSO. Absolutely !—Solid as a rock !

ALBERTO (*encircling* TOMASSO'S *shoulders affectionately*). And all that worry for nothing, eh ? (*Laughs delightedly, then continues more gravely.*) But, doesn't it just show you ?

TOMASSO. What ?

ALBERTO. How right I was to . . .

(*Enter* MARINA (A) *from* R. *She is dressed for the street, but carries her hat. She is hurried and excited, but is trying hard to conceal the fact. The men are standing with their backs to her.*)

ALBERTO (*cont.*) . . . call her bluff ! (*Laughs.*)

TOMASSO (*laughing*). Well, I must say, it seems to.

MARINA (*going straight down* L.) Is that your taxi outside, Tomasso ?

(*The laughter dies on* ALBERTO'S *lips. He does not turn, but remains transfixed.*)

TOMASSO (*turning sharply*). What ?

MARINA (*faintly impatient*). The taxi outside, dear !—Is it yours ? (*Begins to put on hat before mirror.*)

TOMASSO. Yes.—I'd forgotten it.

MARINA. Will you be wanting it again ?

TOMASSO (*looks doubtfully at* ALBERTO). Erm . . . !

MARINA. Now that we're not going to the flower-show ?

TOMASSO. Only to go home !

MARINA. Well, you won't be going yet, will you—so may I have it, please ?

(ALBERTO, *stony faced, still remains with his back to her.*)

TOMASSO (*being awkward—moving towards* MARINA). Matter of fact—I was just going.

MARINA (*meticulously arranging hat and hair*). Oh, then, perhaps you'd drop me off. It won't take you out of your way.

TOMASSO (*uncomfortably*). We—er—we thought you'd gone to bed.

MARINA. Oh, that was just to get rid of that fool Tina. (*Indicates phone.*)

ALBERTO (*without turning*). *What* won't take him out of his way ?

MARINA. The Foro Romano, dear. I've *sud*denly remembered that I promised to meet Mother at the Arch of Settimius at half-past four and—and—and take her for a walk.

ALBERTO. I see.—Will you be long ?

MARINA. Well, I—(*gives a little, nervous laugh*)—I don't know, really. It depends on—how far I'm expected to go.

ALBERTO (*murmuring cryptically*). Yes—quite !

MARINA (*her toilet completed, turns to* TOMASSO). Well—I don't want to hurry you, dear, but . . . (*Breaks off, edging towards archway.*)

TOMASSO (*looks questioningly at* ALBERTO). What about it ?

ALBERTO (*turning for the first time*). Tomasso—I want you to do me the favour of refusing to take my wife to the Foro Romano.

MARINA (*halting in surprise*). What ?

TOMASSO. Very well, Alberto !

ALBERTO (*going to* TOMASSO). If my wife wants to go to the Foro Romano, she can find her own conveyance—or walk.

TOMASSO. As you say, Alberto !

ALBERTO. Good-afternoon, Tomasso ! (*Holds out his hand.*) And thank you !

TOMASSO (*shaking hands*). I wish I could do more. (*Turns, marches to archway, halts, bows slightly and coldly to* MARINA.) Good-afternoon, Marina !

(*Exit* TOMASSO (A) *and to* L.)

MARINA (*resentfully flabbergasted*). What *is* this tomfoolery ?

ALBERTO. I want to talk to you.

MARINA. But I've *told* you, I'm in a *hurry*.—Can't it wait ?

ALBERTO. No, it can *not* wait.

MARINA. Alberto, I *can't* leave the poor old thing standing there like that. You *know* how she suffers with her feet.

ALBERTO. I'm completely callous about your mother's feet.— Come here !

MARINA. But, Alberto . . . !

ALBERTO (*interrupting loudly*). Come *here !*

(MARINA, *intimidated, but still anxious about the time, moves reluctantly to chair,* L.C.)

Sit down !

(MARINA *sits abruptly on arm of chair.* ALBERTO, *his manner softening, moves to her.*)

Marina—just now I asked you to come with me to Ostia. We were interrupted and you—didn't get a chance to reply.

MARINA (*uncomfortably*). Well—it was very sweet of you dear, but—can't we talk about that to-morrow ?

ALBERTO (*flaring up again—shouting*). To-morrow we may not be talking at *all*. (*Turns away,* R.)

MARINA (*startled*). What *is* the matter with you ?

ALBERTO (*regaining control*). I'm sorry.

MARINA. Aren't you well ?

ALBERTO (*bravely*). Oh, I'm—all right, but—— (*Breaks off.*)

MARINA (*concerned*). But what, dear ?

ALBERTO (*suddenly becoming pitiful*). I think I'm a little lonely.

MARINA (*rising and moving to him—compassionately*). Oh— you poor lamb ! (*Puts a hand on his shoulder.*)

ALBERTO. I seem to want—someone to talk to.

MARINA (*kindly*). Well, look—I tell you what—give Tomasso time to get home, then ring him up and ask him to come back again !

ALBERTO. But it's not Tomasso I . . . (*Breaks off and turns to her.*) Marina—I beg of you—I im*plore* you—come with me to Ostia !—Come to-night !—Come now !—*Please !*

MARINA. But how *can* I come now, dear, with poor Mother standing wait . . .

ALBERTO (*interrupting irritably*). Oh, don't keep on talking about your mother ! You know perfectly well she won't be there.

MARINA (*indignantly*). Of *course* she'll be there if she says she will.

ALBERTO. Look ! I'll get the car out and go and *fetch* your mother—and bring her home to *supper*. Will *that* do ?

MARINA. No, of *course* it won't. (*To hide her discomfiture, moves away to mirror and takes out lipstick.*)

ALBERTO. Why not ?

MARINA. Well—she wants the *ex*ercise. (*Begins applying lipstick.*)

ALBERTO. All *right*, then ! *I*'ll take her for a walk. You don't *like* walking. I *do*. You can go to bed and *I*'ll exercise her. How do you like that idea ?

MARINA. I think it's a perfectly idiotic one.

ALBERTO. Exactly! So, shut up about your mother! (*Flops fuming into chair,* L.C.)

MARINA. Is that all, then?

ALBERTO. I suppose so.

(MARINA *moves towards archway, putting away lipstick.*)

Except that . . . (*Breaks off.*)

MARINA (*halting and turning*). Well?

ALBERTO. I think you might have the decency not to stand there making yourself *up*—at *least* not in front of *me*, when you're going out to meet another man.

MARINA (*in a small voice*). What did you say?

ALBERTO. I said " another man." I might have said an anonymous blackguard whose name you don't even know.

MARINA. Oh!

ALBERTO. Yes, " oh! "

(MARINA *moves down to* L. *of couch.*)

MARINA. So you know about that!

ALBERTO. I know *all* about it.

MARINA. Oh—I see! (*Stands in thought.*)

ALBERTO (*waits a moment*). Well?

MARINA (*angrily*). Well, I do think you might have said something sooner, instead of letting me stand here and tell a lot of stupid lies about my mother.

ALBERTO (*in astonishment*). Is that all you've got to say?

MARINA. There's not much I *can* say, is there—if you know all about it?

ALBERTO (*rising and facing her*). But aren't you *sorry* or a*shamed* or *any*thing?

MARINA. I'm sorry, of course.—I've worried a *lot* about you.

ALBERTO. Oh!—thanks!

MARINA. But I've nothing to be a*shamed* of. It's a very beautiful thing.

ALBERTO (*cryptically*). *I* know how beautiful it is.

MARINA. And I've done *nothing wrong*.

ALBERTO. No, I know you haven't.

MARINA. Well, I'm glad you give me *that* much credit.

ALBERTO. You haven't had the chance.

MARINA (*stiffly*).   I *beg* your pardon !

ALBERTO (*crossing*).   And what's more, you *won't* have, if only you knew it.   (*Sits couch.*)

MARINA (*haughtily*).   I don't know what you mean by that, but in any case it's not a question of " having a chance " as you call it, because it's not that kind of association at all.

ALBERTO (*sarcastically*).   No ?

MARINA.   No.   It's pure in a way which would be entirely beyond your comprehension.

ALBERTO.   I see.

MARINA.   And I shall be *very* much surprised if it doesn't re*main* so.

ALBERTO.   Not half as surprised as *I* shall be.

MARINA.   Well, you're evidently bent on being cryptic, and I'm afraid I haven't the time to waste in finding out what you're talking about, so—if you don't mind, I'll . . . (*Breaks off and moves towards archway.*)

ALBERTO.   You're going, then ?

MARINA.   Certainly I'm going.

ALBERTO.   Even if I . . . (*hesitates*).

MARINA (*halting*).   What ?

ALBERTO.   . . . ask you not to ?

MARINA.   I'm afraid so, Alberto.

ALBERTO.   Even though I tell you that I'm—prepared to be generous ?

MARINA.   Generous ?

ALBERTO.   And overlook it !—Forget he ever existed !

MARINA.   *You* might be able to.—I *never* could.

ALBERTO.   All right, then !   Don't let me keep you !

MARINA.   Besides, I've got *him* to consider—and he's very sensitive.   I don't know *what* he'd do.

ALBERTO (*sarcastically*).   Oh, well—that settles it.

MARINA (*lingering*).   So, you see, I . . .

ALBERTO (*interrupting*).   Get *on* with it, then !   You can't keep him waiting.   The poor fellow may suffer with his feet too—for all you know about him.

(MARINA *still lingers.   As she looks at the sulky figure of her husband, her expression softens.*)

MARINA (*comes down to behind sofa—kindly*).   I *am* sorry, Alberto.   I am really.   I wouldn't have had it happen for worlds.

But—you *must* understand that it's—that it's something beyond my control. It's bigger than I am.

ALBERTO (*folds his arms and laughs bitterly and shortly*). Huh!

MARINA. You see, dear . . . (*Breaks off.*) I don't want to hurt you, but it's better to be open and honest, isn't it?

ALBERTO. Oh, *much* better!

MARINA. Well, you see—*he* gives me something that I don't think you could even understand—a sense of spiritual completeness—a feeling of the *oneness* of—of our . . .

ALBERTO (*interpolating*). Souls!

MARINA. Yes—and the absolute knowledge that we were . . .

ALBERTO (*interpolating*). Pre-destined!

MARINA. Yes—that's the very word he . . . (*Breaks off.*)— How do *you* know all this?

ALBERTO. That's my business.

MARINA. And, come to think of it—how do you know I don't even know his name?

ALBERTO. Well—you may as well know! (*Rises, moves to* R. *of couch and faces her.*) Perhaps I can make you look silly, if I can't do anything else.—I've seen his letters.

MARINA (*incredulously*). You've seen his . . . ?

ALBERTO (*interrupting*). Yes, and . . .

MARINA (*interrupting*). You mean you've been reading my . . .

ALBERTO (*interrupting*). Yes, and of all the miserable, sentimental slush . . .

MARINA (*interrupting furiously*). You *cow*ard!

ALBERTO. How on earth a woman like you could . . .

MARINA (*interrupting*). How *dare* you open my private correspondence?

ALBERTO. . . . could be bamboozled by . . .

MARINA (*interrupting—advancing on him*). And to *think* that I've *lived* with you *all* these years without knowing what sort of a man you were!

ALBERTO (*backing away*). Now, look here, it's no use you . . .

MARINA (*interrupting*). And I suppose you've been doing it ever since we were *married!*

ALBERTO (*still backing*). No, I . . .

MARINA (*interrupting*). Steaming open envelopes! Two or three a day!

(ALBERTO, *having reached chair down* R., *falls into it.* MARINA *stands over him.*)

Reading about Mother's symptoms—or what Tina thinks of the woman in the flat below—for twenty years—without *finding* anything ! What doggedness ! What singleness of purpose !— Well, I hope you're satisfied—even if it's taken you hundreds of man-hours and thousands of gallons of boiling water to get what you wanted. (*Pauses for breath.*) And, incidentally, if you think there's anything about *that* revelation to make *me* look silly . . .! (*Breaks off as——*)

(BERNARDO'S *familiar whistle is heard, off.* ALBERTO, *to whom this has no significance, takes no notice. But* MARINA'S *eyes open wide in a kind of thrilled horror.*)

(*After slight pause*). I must go ! (*Turns and runs out.*)

(*Exit* MARINA (A) *and to* L.)

ALBERTO (*jumping to his feet in great dismay*). Marina ! (*Hurries after her.*) Marina ! (*Runs out.*)

(*Exit* ALBERTO (A) *and to* L.)

(BERNARDO'S *face appears at window, up* R. *Enter* ROSINA, L. BERNARDO *at once makes signals meaning* " *have you got them ?* " ROSINA *puts a finger to her lips enjoining caution and remains in doorway, listening.*

Front door slams, off. ROSINA *nods to* BERNARDO *and bobs out.*

Exit ROSINA (L).

Enter BERNARDO (F.W.). *He hesitates warily in doorway.*

Front door slams again, off.

Reassured, BERNARDO *at once crosses with confidence to meet* ROSINA. *Enter* ROSINA, L. *She carries an enormous armful of red roses in all stages of development.*)

ROSINA (*in a conspiratorial tone*). Here they are !
BERNARDO. Good ! (*Takes them from her.*) How many ?
ROSINA. Three lots ! Six dozen !

BERNARDO. Is that all you've got ?

ROSINA. Oh, no ! This is only about half. But some of the others are getting on a bit.

BERNARDO. Never mind ! Let's have 'em. There are plenty of people with defective sight.

ROSINA (*starts to go out—checks herself*). But—what about . . . ? (*Hesitates.*)

BERNARDO. We'll talk about that later. I've got to sell 'em first. (*Pushes her with his hip.*) Go on ! Get 'em !

(*Exit* ROSINA, L.)

(BERNARDO *begins singing softly.* ALBERTO *is seen to pass window, up* R. *Enter* ALBERTO, F.W. *Looking bitter and savage, he halts on seeing the unaware* BERNARDO.)

ALBERTO. What do *you* want ?

BERNARDO (*turns with a start*). Oh, I—I . . . (*Hesitates at a loss.*)

ALBERTO (*moving to* C.). What are you doing here ?

BERNARDO (*thinking fast*). I was hoping to see you, Signor.

ALBERTO. Well ?

BERNARDO. I—I just brought these up. (*Indicates roses.*)

ALBERTO. What for ?

BERNARDO. Well, they're an—odd lot, and—I got them a little cheap, and—knowing that you—knew someone who liked red roses, I . . .

(ALBERTO, *looking very formidable, advances slowly on* BERNARDO.)

(*Faltering more than ever and backing a little*) . . . I thought that—you might perhaps—like to . . . (*Trails off altogether as* ALBERTO *confronts him.*)

ALBERTO (*stands looking down at roses for a brief moment in sullen consideration*). Got any more ?

BERNARDO (*in surprise*). More ?

ALBERTO (*fiercely*). *Yes—more !*

BERNARDO (*with a glance at door,* L.). I—I think I know where I could *get* some.

ALBERTO (*suddenly taking roses from* BERNARDO). Right ! Get 'em !

BERNARDO. They may not be quite as fresh as these, Signor.

ALBERTO. I don't care! Get 'em! Many as you like!— Now, get out! (*Moves to* c.)

BERNARDO (*scuttling for door*). Yes, Signor! Thank you, Signor.

(*Exit* BERNARDO, F.W.)

ALBERTO (*shouts*). Rosina! (*Stands a moment—bellows.*) Rosina!

(*Enter* ROSINA, L.)

ROSINA (*startled—timidly*). Yes, Signor?
ALBERTO (*holding out flowers*). Put these in water!

ROSINA'S *face takes on an expression of profound amazement as she advances to comply.*)

CURTAIN

ACT III

SCENE : *The same, late that evening.*

(*Curtain rises on an empty stage. A number of vases of all shapes and sizes, filled with red roses in all stages of development, now occupy every vantage point in the room. There is also an atmosphere of disorder. The writing desk is a confusion of papers and its drawers lie open. Several articles of male apparel (including a pile of shirts on back of couch) lie about the furniture. ALBERTO'S jacket is draped over the back of chair, L.C. A small suitcase, containing books and papers, lies open on the back of couch, and a large and very full suitcase stands open down R. The French-windows are open. It is dark outside, and the curtains (except those of F.W.) are drawn. The room is fully lit.*)

BERNARDO'S *whistle is heard, off.*

Enter ALBERTO, *followed by* ROSINA (A) *from* R. ALBERTO, *who still looks sullen and ill-tempered is in his shirt-sleeves and carries a brief-case. He wears the same suit as in Act II. He strides straight across to desk.* ROSINA, *having almost to run to keep up, follows with a pile comprising several books, some ties and a hot-water bottle.*)

ALBERTO (*sitting at desk*). Put 'em in there, will you ? (*Indicates small suitcase and at once begins sorting papers.*)

(ROSINA *begins to comply, and for a moment they work in silence.*)

ROSINA (*in a worried tone*). I can't *think* what's happened to the Signora.
                    (ALBERTO *does not reply.*)

She's been gone nearly four hours.

(*Still no reply from* ALBERTO *who is putting papers in brief-case.*)

Signor !

ALBERTO. Um ?

ROSINA (*shutting down suitcase lid*). I say I do hope nothing's happened to the . . .

ALBERTO (*interrupting*). I know. I heard you. (*Indicates her suitcase.*) Shove that in the hall, will you ?

(ROSINA *starts with suitcase for archway.*)

And then come back and help me shut that trunk !

(*Exit* ROSINA (A) *and to* L.)

(ALBERTO *continues for a moment sorting papers and putting them in brief-case. Then he rises and starts for archway. As he does so,* BERNARDO'S *whistle is heard again.*)

(*Changes his direction to* F.W., *leans out and bellows*). Shut-up !

(*The whistle stops abruptly.* ALBERTO *continues across. Front door bell rings, off.* ALBERTO *halts, pauses listening, then continues off.*
          Exit ALBERTO (A) *and to* R.)

ROSINA (*off*). But have you had anything to eat ?

MARINA (*off*). Yes, I've had a sandwich, thank you !

(*Enter* MARINA *and* ROSINA (A.) *from* L.)

ROSINA (*almost severely*). We were getting quite worried about you. Did anything happen ?

MARINA (*coming down,* L. *of couch, pulling off her hat*). No, nothing at all ! I—er—I expected to meet someone, that's all and he—er—and she didn't turn up. So I—(*giggling nervously*)—so I took myself to the pictures.

ROSINA. Oh !

MARINA. Rather a silly thing in technicolor called . . . (*Turning, breaks off as she sees flowers, surveys them in astonishment.*) What on earth . . . ? (*Breaks off.*)

ROSINA (*looking grave*). The roses, you mean ?

MARINA. Yes.

ROSINA. Signor Verani bought them.

MARINA.   My *hus*band ?

ROSINA.   Yes, Signora.

MARINA.   But—but *why ?*   What's the *point* of it ?   Is it a *joke ?*

ROSINA.   Well, *I* should have thought it was a joke, only . . . (*Breaks off.*)

MARINA.   Only what ?

ROSINA.   He doesn't seem to be in a joking mood.

MARINA.   No—and even if he were, it wouldn't be *ter*ribly funny, would it ?

ROSINA.   No.

MARINA (*surveying the mess*).   And the *room*, Rosina !

ROSINA (*looking more worried than ever*).   I know.

MARINA.   What *has* he been doing ?

ROSINA.   Well, I couldn't quite make out at first, but I finally came to the conclusion that he was packing.

MARINA (*in surprise*).   *Pack*ing ?

(*Enter* ALBERTO (A.) *from* R.   *He carries a bag of golf-clubs, one shoe and a soft, felt hat.*)

ALBERTO (*walking straight across to* R. *of couch, throws a cold glance at* MARINA).   Good-evening !

MARINA.   Good-evening !

(*Exit* ROSINA, L.)

(*There is an unfriendly silence during which* ALBERTO *stuffs shoe into golf bag, and* MARINA *eyes him covertly.*)

ALBERTO (*ironically*).   Have a good time ?

MARINA.   Oh, lovely, thank you !

ALBERTO (*faintly surprised*).   You did ?

MARINA.   Why shouldn't I ?

ALBERTO (*puzzled*).   No reason at all, only . . . (*Breaks off.*) What have you been doing, then'?

MARINA (*vaguely*).   Oo—dancing a little and . . .

ALBERTO (*interrupting*).   Dancing !   Who with ?

MARINA.   You know as well as I do, who with !

ALBERTO.   Are you—are you trying to tell me that you—met this fellow after all ?

MARINA.   Certainly I met him.

ALBERTO (*looks at her almost admiringly*). Well, I'm damned !

MARINA. What's so strange about that ?

ALBERTO. Nothing !—Nothing at all ! (*Begins rolling up hat and stuffing it into golf bag.*)

MARINA. Well, then . . . ! (*Sits arm of chair* L.C. *watching him.*)

ALBERTO. You weren't late, I hope, for your appointment ? (*Props golf-bag behind couch and moves to desk.*)

MARINA. Well, I was, rather.

ALBERTO (*sits at desk*). Oh !—I *am* sorry ! (*Begins searching for something.*)

MARINA (*loftily*). Not at all ! It didn't matter in the least.

ALBERTO. He waited ?

MARINA. Of *course* he waited.

ALBERTO. Well—that's *always* a good sign.

MARINA (*faintly irritable*). Are you looking for something ?

ALBERTO. Labels !

MARINA. Top, left-hand drawer !

ALBERTO (*opens drawer*). Ah ! Thank you ! (*Takes out labels and at once begins looking for something else.*) You have dined, I suppose ?

MARINA. We dined at the Plaza.

ALBERTO (*with raised eyebrows*). The *Plaza* !—Spreading himself, eh ?

MARINA (*getting a little uncomfortable and haughty*). Not at all ! He *lives* there.

ALBERTO (*in a gratified tone*). Oh—rich !

MARINA. I should think so—very !

ALBERTO (*still searching*). Commerce, I suppose !

MARINA. Then you suppose *quite* wrong.

ALBERTO (*distastefully*). Not trade, surely ?

MARINA (*coldly*). He has estates and things, if you want to know—in the country—*family* ones !

ALBERTO. Better and better !—You haven't seen my fountain-pen, have you ?

MARINA (*shortly*). *Bottom*—left !

ALBERTO. Oh—thank you ! (*Finds pen.*) And how about his personal appearance ?

MARINA (*increasingly uncomfortable*). His . . . ? (*Hesitates.*)

ALBERTO. Yes. Did it come up to your expectations—or hopes, rather ? (*Begins writing label.*)

MARINA (*rising haughtily*). I find that rather offensive, Alberto.

ALBERTO. I'm sorry. I'm being indelicate. Any children ?

MARINA. *Children* ! *No !* He's not even *married*.

ALBERTO. That wasn't quite the question.

MARINA. Well, don't you think that some of these questions—coming from you—are a little odd—in the circumstances ?

ALBERTO. Not half as odd as some of the answers.

MARINA (*trying to put up a bold front*). If you think I'm exaggerating . . . !

ALBERTO. I think you're lying yourself black in the face, my dear.

MARINA (*loftily*). Well—I'm not going to be drawn into an undignified argument about *that*, I can assure you.—But I should be glad if you'd tell *me* something.

ALBERTO. With pleasure !

MARINA (*crosses to him*). Did you get these ?

(ALBERTO *looks round and* MARINA *indicates roses.*)

ALBERTO (*turning back again*). I did.

MARINA. Why ?

ALBERTO (*turning again in apparent surprise*). *Why !*

MARINA. Yes. What's the idea ?

ALBERTO. I thought you *liked* red roses.

MARINA. I do—normally.

ALBERTO. Don't you like these ?

MARINA. No !

ALBERTO. Why not ?

MARINA. Because I think you got them in a silly temper. (*Goes to coffee-table.*)

ALBERTO. I see. (*Turns back to desk.*)

MARINA. To an*noy* me. (*Takes a cigarette.*)

ALBERTO. Put it like that if you wish !

MARINA. How *else* could you put it ? (*Picks up matches and lights cigarette.*)

(*Front door bell rings, off.*)

ALBERTO (*puts down pen, rises and goes to her—with dignity*). Marina—the roses are something for you to remember me by.

MARINA. Uh ?

ALBERTO. I'm getting out.

(MARINA, *suddenly transfixed, drops matchbox on table.*)

I suppose you realise that?

MARINA. I beg your pardon?

ALBERTO. I'm leaving you, Marina.

MARINA (*incredulously*). You're *leaving* me?

ALBERTO. Quite definitely! If I had any doubts up to five minutes ago—you yourself have removed them.

MARINA (*staggered*). But, what . . . ?

ALBERTO (*interrupting loudly*). And *don't* behave as if you can't think of anything to account for it! But if you *want* a reason, I'll *give* you one.—I don't *like* you! (*Turns, nearly falls over suitcase, goes back to desk, sits and begins writing again.*)

MARINA (*stands for a moment looking dazed*). Oh!—I see! (*Turning slowly away.*) Well, I—I think I'll go and get into something comfortable. (*Moves towards archway.*)

ALBERTO (*unfeelingly*). I should!

(*Enter* TOMASSO (A.) *from* L. *He wears the same suit as in Act II, and carries a hat.* MARINA *and* TOMASSO *halt as they confront each other.*)

MARINA (*trying to speak in everyday tones—politely surprised*). Oh!—Tomasso!

(ALBERTO *glances round, then continues writing.*)

TOMASSO (*awkwardly*). Good-evening, Marina! Just going out?

MARINA. No, I've—just come in. (*Laughs nervously.*)

TOMASSO. Oh! (*Laughs nervously.*)

MARINA. Lovely out, isn't it?

TOMASSO. Lovely!

MARINA (*miserably*). Everything looking so gay!

TOMASSO. Rather!

MARINA. Lots of people about, too!

TOMASSO. Yes, indeed!

MARINA. But the *traffic*, my dear!

TOMASSO. Oh—awful!

MARINA. Yes. (*Suddenly her face crumples. She bursts into tears and rushes off.*)

(*Exit* MARINA (A.) *and to* R.)

(TOMASSO *stares after her in astonishment.* ALBERTO *puts down his pen, but does not turn.*)

TOMASSO (*turning to* ALBERTO, *angrily*). *Now* what have you been doing ?

ALBERTO (*sullenly*). I'm leaving her, that's all !

TOMASSO. You mean—for *good ?*

ALBERTO. That's what I mean.

TOMASSO (*putting his hat on cabinet*). But—on the phone just now you said . . .

ALBERTO (*interrupting querulously*). *I* know. *I* know.

TOMASSO. I thought we'd got it all fixed.

ALBERTO. That was a couple of hours ago.

TOMASSO. Well, what's happened since ?

ALBERTO. I've realised that going away for just a few weeks isn't going to do any good, that's all.

TOMASSO. Why not ?

ALBERTO. Simply because she's *never* going to hear from this fellow *again.*

TOMASSO. What a*bout* it ?

ALBERTO (*rises—turns argumentatively*). Look ! From now on he drops her, doesn't he ?

TOMASSO. Yes, that's what we arranged.

ALBERTO (*interrupting*). No flowers ! No notes ! No letters ! *Noth*ing !

TOMASSO. That's right ! (*Moving* L.) And the whole point about you going away was so that you wouldn't have to see the sad look in her eyes while she was getting over it. (*Sits arm of chair*, L.C.)

ALBERTO. Right ! Now !—Supposing she *does* get over it . . . !

TOMASSO. Yes ?

ALBERTO. Do you think that's going to finish the whole thing ?

TOMASSO. Well, I suppose so.

ALBERTO. Don't you believe it ! (*Going to him—impressively.*) Do you know what she did this evening ?

TOMASSO. What ?

ALBERTO. Spent nearly four hours with him !

TOMASSO. Uh ?

ALBERTO.   *Dan*ced with him !

TOMASSO.   But—but she couldn't have.

ALBERTO.   I *know* she couldn't have—but she *said* she *did !*

TOMASSO.   But why on earth should she say a thing like that ?

ALBERTO.   Simply because she wasn't going to admit that he'd stood her up !

TOMASSO.   Oh, I see !

ALBERTO.   So, d'you think she could ever bring herself to admit that he'd *chucked* her altogether ?

TOMASSO.   You're not suggesting that—(*rises*)—that she'd keep the man going indefinitely—just to impress *you ?*

ALBERTO.   She's quite capable of it, believe me.—Anyway, I'm not going to risk it. (*Turns away, picks up shirts from back of couch and takes them to suitcase down* R.)

TOMASSO (*going to behind couch*). Can't you appeal to her sense of heroism ?

ALBERTO.   Eh ?

TOMASSO.   Ask her to give him up and let it look as if she's *sac*rificing herself.

ALBERTO.   I *have* asked her.   She hasn't *got* a sense of heroism. (*Puts shirts into suitcase and tramples them down.*)

TOMASSO.   What did she say ?

ALBERTO.   Said he'd got something *I* hadn't got. (*Goes to desk and picks up a label.*)

TOMASSO.   Then, for heaven's sake, why don't you just *tell* her ?

ALBERTO (*returning*).   Tell her what ?   (*Begins tying label on suitcase.*)

TOMASSO.   That the man never existed.

ALBERTO.   How can I do that without letting her know it was me ?

TOMASSO.   Then, *let* her know !

ALBERTO (*pauses in his work—horrified*).   *What !*

TOMASSO.   Con*fess*, man !

ALBERTO.   *Af*ter *all this ?*   She'd never for*give* me !

TOMASSO.   I can't see that tnat 'ud be any worse than the way it is.

ALBERTO.   On the contrary—if there's got to be one of us not forgiving the other, I'd rather it was *me*. (*Finishes tying label*.)   Did you get the money ?

TOMASSO (*gloomily*).   Yes.   (*Takes roll of notes from his pocket and moves to* ALBERTO.)

ALBERTO. Thanks ! (*Takes his wallet from hip pocket and hands it to* TOMASSO.) Shove 'em in here, will you ? (*Goes up to cocktail cabinet.*)

TOMASSO (*putting notes in wallet*). I suppose there's no point in saying so now, but you did ask me to meet you with it at the Station.

ALBERTO (*in the act of taking a bottle from cabinet, is arrested, horrified*). Oh, my God ! So I did !

TOMASSO (*moving to desk*). At seven o'clock !

ALBERTO. You didn't *go*, did you ?

TOMASSO. Of *course* I went. (*Throws wallet on desk.*)

ALBERTO. I'm *ter*ribly sorry, old chap ! (*Taking bottle to suitcase.*) I expected to get an earlier train.

TOMASSO. Where are you going, anyway ?

ALBERTO. Turin ! I have friends there. (*Puts bottle in suitcase and shuts it down.*)

TOMASSO. Oh ! (*Watches in a distressed way*).

ALBERTO (*straightens up and pauses considering*). Let me see ! I'm sure there was something else I had to do.

TOMASSO. Meet me at the Station half-an-hour ago !

ALBERTO. Oh, yes, of course ! That's it ! (*Goes off with suitcase, picking up golf-clubs on the way.*)

(*Exit* ALBERTO (A.) *and to* L.)

(*Enter* MARINA (A.) *from* R. *She now wears an attractive loose, semi-evening gown. Moving swiftly into archway, she pauses to peer after* ALBERTO, *giving the impression that she has been waiting for this opportunity.*)

MARINA (*going to* TOMASSO—*looking very distressed*). Tomasso ! (*Holds out both hands to him.*)

TOMASSO (*moving to meet her*). My dear ! (*Takes her hands.*)

MARINA. Has he told you ?

(TOMASSO *nods.*)

Isn't it awful ?

(TOMASSO *nods.*)

D'you think it's unbalanced him—all this worry ?

TOMASSO. Unbalanced him ? *No !*

MARINA. But it's so un*like* him—-to leave me.—He's always been such a home-lover.

TOMASSO (*urging her gently towards couch*). Come and sit down !

MARINA. And he's acting so *strange*ly. (*Indicating the state of the room.*) Look at all . . . (*Breaks off as——*)

(*Enter* ALBERTO (A.) *from* L. *He pounds straight across archway carrying a weird assortment of objects, including a hold-all, tennis racket, rug, pneumatic cushion, shooting stick, etc.*

Exit ALBERTO (A.) *to* R.)

You see ?—I've never *known* him go on like this before.

TOMASSO (*kindly*). But, after all, Marina—what do you expect ?

MARINA (*getting tearful*). I don't know. (*Fumbles for handkerchief and sinks into couch.*)

TOMASSO (*gently*). I mean, you *are* playing around with somebody else, *are*n't you ?

MARINA. There's nothing *play*ful about it, Tomasso, **really**.

TOMASSO (*sitting beside her*). I dare say—but still . . .

MARINA (*interrupting—suddenly giving way*). Oh, I know ! I'm just pretending to myself, that's all. Of *course* he's right to leave me. (*Weeping freely.*) What decent man's going to stand for that sort of thing ?

TOMASSO. You don't want him to go, do you ?

(MARINA *shakes her head.*)

Then why don't you renounce this chap, Marina ?

MARINA. I've *tried* to, I have really—but I just **can't**. I don't seem able to face the future without him.

TOMASSO. You mean you—really and truly love him.

MARINA. I don't *know*. And the awful thing is—I don't think I ever *shall* know—until I meet him.

TOMASSO (*deeply impressed*). Oh, dear !

MARINA. That's why I was so disappointed when he wasn't there to-day. I was half hoping that he'd have a squint and bad teeth or something—because then the spell might have been broken, and I could have come back to Alberto and told him I was sorry, and . . . (*Breaks off.*)

(*Enter* ALBERTO (A.) *from* R. *He enters hurriedly, carrying a hat, raincoat, umbrella and small bag. These he deposits in chair* L.C., *then, taking his jacket from the back of it, begins hastily to put it on.* TOMASSO *rises slowly and stands watching him* (R. *of couch*). MARINA, *sitting with bent head, tries to remove the traces of her tears.*)

TOMASSO. You're off, then ?

ALBERTO (*struggling into jacket*). Yes.—You haven't got a taxi outside, have you ?

TOMASSO (*glad to be able to say it*). No. I walked here.

ALBERTO. Well, would you mind getting me one ?

TOMASSO. No, I'm damned if I . . .

MARINA (*interrupting—gently*). Get him one, dear !

TOMASSO. Oh, very well ! (*Goes reluctantly to archway—to* ALBERTO.) You don't want me to come to the Station, do you ?

ALBERTO. Well, I thought, perhaps—Marina might like you to stay with her for a bit. (*Picks up hat, coat, bag and umbrella.*)

TOMASSO. I was only going to say I wasn't going to, that's all.

(*Exit* TOMASSO (A.) *and to* L.)

ALBERTO (*now ready to leave, throws a worried glance at* MARINA *and hesitates uncomfortably*). Er—would you mind sending on my trunk ?

MARINA (*pathetically brave*). Certainly !

ALBERTO. I wouldn't bother you only—I'm a bit pressed for time.

MARINA (*with a faint, twisted little smile*). It's no bother.

ALBERTO. Thanks !—There *is* a label on it.

MARINA. Oh !

ALBERTO (*pauses awkwardly*). You—er—you needn't worry about money, or anything. I've seen to that.

MARINA. Thank you, Alberto !

(*Front door slams, off.*)

ALBERTO. And if you want anything done at any time—I'm sure Tomasso would be only too glad to . . . (*Trails off.*)

MARINA. Oh, I'm *sure* he will.

(*Pause.* MARINA *remains sitting with bent head. Each avoids the other's eye.* ALBERTO, *fiddling nervously with his paraphernalia, gets increasingly entangled with it.*)

ALBERTO. Well—I hope you'll be happy.
MARINA. Thank you ! I hope you will be, too.
ALBERTO. Thank you !
MARINA. Are you going anywhere nice ?
ALBERTO. I thought I'd go to the Brunos in Turin for a bit.
MARINA (*with false cheerfulness*). Oh, well, they're nice people.
ALBERTO. Yes.
MARINA. Nice large town, too !
ALBERTO. Yes.

(*Pause. Each looks increasingly miserable.*)

I—er—I've put a new bulb in your bedside lamp.
MARINA. Oh, thank you ! That's nice.
ALBERTO. And I've wound both the clocks.
MARINA. Oh, you have ! Good !

(*Slight pause.*)

ALBERTO. Well—I can't think of anything else—can you ?
MARINA. No, *I* can't think of anything else.
ALBERTO (*with an effort*). Good-bye, then !
MARINA (*with averted head*). Good-bye !

(ALBERTO *hesitates, then moves in wretched embarrassment to archway.*)

ALBERTO (*halts*). Oh—and I phoned the plumber about that tap.
MARINA. Oh, you did !
ALBERTO. Yes.—Well—good-bye !
MARINA. Good-bye !

(ALBERTO *throws her a glance of anguish, puts on his hat and goes out* (A.) *and to* L.)

(MARINA'S *face takes on an expression of unrestrained woe. She again begins dabbing at her nose with her handkerchief. Enter* ROSINA, L.)

ROSINA (*bobs her head in and glances round*). Has he gone, Signora ?

MARINA. Yes—he's gone.

ROSINA (*coming into the room*). Oh !—He wanted me to sit on his trunk.

(*Front door slams, off.*)

(*In a small voice*) Signora !

MARINA. Um ?

ROSINA. Isn't he coming back ?

MARINA. No.

ROSINA (*deeply impressed*). Never ?

MARINA. No—never ! (*Rises, crosses and sinks into chair at desk.*)

ROSINA (*shocked*). Aooh !—I *thought* he was packing like that. It was the way *cook* packed when *she* left. (*Going to* MARINA—*compassionately.*) Oh, what a *shame !* Oh, I *am* sorry ! (*Puts an arm about* MARINA's *shoulders.*)—Was it on account of the flowers ?

MARINA (*leaning her head against* ROSINA). Yes.

ROSINA. He found out ?

MARINA. Yes.

ROSINA. Oh, *poor* Signora ! Can't I do anything ?

MARINA. No.

ROSINA. Wouldn't you like some coffee ?

MARINA. No, thank you !

ROSINA. A nice *glass* of something, then ?

(MARINA *shakes her head.*)

It 'ud help, you know, if you gave way and had a good cry.

MARINA. I've had one.—It didn't help at all. (*At once begins to cry.*)

ROSINA (*releasing* MARINA—*resentfully*). Well, *I* don't think it's fair.

MARINA (*weeping freely*). Yes, it is.

ROSINA. Why should *you* have to suffer, just because a nasty old man like that . . . ?

MARINA (*interrupting—sitting up shocked*). Rosina !

ROSINA (*backing away a little*). Oh, I don't mean *him*, Signora. I mean . . . (*Breaks off.*) But, of course—you don't know about that !

MARINA (*rises, breathing hard*).   Rosina!—*What* don't I know about?

ROSINA.   You're not going to *like* it, Signora.

MARINA (*impatiently*).   *Rosina, please!*

ROSINA.   It's . . . (*Hesitates.*)

MARINA.   *Yes?*

ROSINA.   Well, it's Signor Savelli!

MARINA (*blankly*).   Signor Savelli what?

ROSINA.   Who's been sending the *flowers.*

MARINA (*uncomprehendingly*).   How d'you mean?

ROSINA.   Well—*he's* the one*!*

MARINA.   Rosina, you're crazy!

ROSINA.   *No*, Signora!   I *caught* him at it.

MARINA.   You what?

ROSINA.   This afternoon—when you'd gone to lie down!   I came in here, and there he was—red-handed—just looking for somewhere to put them.

MARINA.   You mean you actually *saw* him bringing them in?

ROSINA.   *Yes*, Signora!

MARINA.   But—it isn't *cre*dible.   I—I mean, I've known him for twenty-one *years.*   He's always been most re*spect*ful.

ROSINA.   They do go funny, you know.   (*Goes to* F.W. *and looks out to her right.*)

MARINA (*gesticulating in sudden resentment—crossing*).   *Oh*, it's *too* bad, it is *real*ly.   They *are* the most unpre*dic*table creatures.   You never know where you *are* with them.   Either they leave you or they don't keep appointments, or else they do *this* sort of thing.—(*Halts abruptly*, R.C.)   But, Rosina!

ROSINA (*turning from* F.W.).   Yes, Signora?

MARINA.   If it *was* Savelli—that means that there *isn't* any other one.

ROSINA.   Not the way you pictured him, anyway.

MARINA (*stricken*).   Ooh!

ROSINA (*looking out of* F.W. *again*).   The taxi's come.

MARINA.   Oh, and he was *so* lovely, Rosina.

ROSINA (*turning*).   It's no good grieving over somebody who never existed, Signora.

MARINA.   But it's so *sad.*   It seems so pitiful to think that all that love—that splendid spirit—that warm, generous nature was—nothing more than a dream—or rather was nothing more than that stupid oaf Savelli playing the fool.

ROSINA (*sympathetically*).   I know.   It *is* sad.

MARINA. And he under*stood* me so well.—Better than anybody's ever done before. It just doesn't seem possible that . . . (*Breaks off.*) But, Rosina !

ROSINA. Yes, Signora ?

MARINA. *If* he never existed—that means that—that I'm losing my husband for *noth*ing.

ROSINA (*turning back to* F.W.). If you *let* him go—yes.

MARINA. What do you mean, if I let him go ? How can I prevent it ?

ROSINA (*hurrying to* MARINA). You *might* catch him. (*Trying to urge* MARINA *out.*) He's just getting his things into the cab.

MARINA (*getting agitated*). But what could I *tell* him if I *did ?*

ROSINA (*pushing* MARINA, L.). The truth, Signora !

MARINA. That it was Savelli ?

ROSINA. Of course !

MARINA. But, he's his *best friend*, Rosina. He'd *kill* him.

ROSINA. It's no good considering other people *too* much. (*Returns again to* F.W.)

MARINA (*suddenly making for archway*). You're quite right, Rosina. I'll make a clean breast of it, Tomasso or no Tomasso, I'll . . .

ROSINA (*interrupting—turning away from* F.W.). Well, it's gone now, anyway.

MARINA (*halting and returning*). Well—that's that ! (*Sits in resentful self-pity on arm of chair*, L.C.) So my husband's left me—I never had a lover—and now I've got to have a row with the man who's always been like a *fa*ther to me.—Rosina, if it goes on like this, I shan't have *any*one.

ROSINA (*going to* MARINA—*reassuringly*). *I* shan't leave you, Signora.

MARINA (*taking* ROSINA'S *hands*). I know—and you're a pet—but it's not quite the same thing, is it ?

ROSINA (*understandingly*). No.

(*Front door bell rings, off.*)

MARINA (*releasing* ROSINA'S *hands—resentfully*). Ah ! Now the idiot's gone and locked himself out.

ROSINA (*starting towards archway*). Shall I . . . ?

MARINA. No.—Let him wait for a bit ! (*Rises in sudden fury.*) How *dare* he ? How *dare* he think that his beastly flowers and insipid letters should . . . ?

Rosina (*interrupting*).   The thing is—what are you going to do about it ?

Marina.   Well, I suppose the first thing to do is to get him to admit it.

Rosina.   He'll never do that now—not after all this—unless, of course . . . (*Hesitates.*)

Marina.   What ?

Rosina.   Unless you like to let him think you wouldn't *mind*.

Marina.   Mind what ?

Rosina.   If it *did* turn out to be him.

Marina (*quite aghast*).   You mean . . . ?   (*Breaks off.*)

Rosina.   Yes.

Marina.   Encourage him ?

Rosina.   Just for the time being—yes.

Marina.   Make advances to him ?

Rosina.   It's the only way you'll . . . (*Breaks off as——*)

(*Front door bell rings, off.*)

Marina (*crossing to* R.C.).   Oh, how *dare* he put me in such a position ?   How *dare* he take it upon himself to . . . ?

Rosina (*interrupting*).   Shall I let him in then ?

Marina.   *I* suppose so.

(Rosina *hurries off* (A.) *and to* L.)

(Marina *stands champing in angry thought for a moment, then hurries to electric switch* (R. *of archway*) *and turns out main lights so that the room is lit only by the table lamps. She then goes to mirror, rapidly dabs her hair, pauses to think again, turns to radiogram, opens it, quickly selects a record* (*something dreamy and sentimental*), *puts it on, runs across to couch and settles herself* (*after some experiment*) *in an attitude of studied grace. All this is done with an air of petulant anger.*)

(*Enter* Rosina (A.) *from* L.)

Rosina.   Wasn't there.   I expect he's coming up the side way.   (*Looks upwards.*)   Something wrong with the lights ?   (*Reaches for switch, turns lights on.*)

(MARINA *stirs impatiently. Enter* TOMASSO, F.W. *He seems deeply preoccupied.*)

ROSINA (*catching on*). Oh! (*Switches lights off again and moves down* L.)

(*Exit* ROSINA, L.)

TOMASSO (*coming out of his abstraction for a moment, moves down to behind couch*). My dear!—Don't grieve so!

(MARINA *clenches her fists and a spasm of fury passes over her face.*)

(*Comes round couch, sits beside her and takes her hand*). If only there were something I could do!

(MARINA *snatches away her hand, rises, goes upstage and stands with her back turned, fuming.*)

(*Sympathetically*). I know!—It's rotten, isn't it?

(*At this point the record, a cracked one, begins to repeat and continues to do so.* MARINA, *apparently unconscious of this, turns, glaring at* TOMASSO's *backview. With an effort she wipes the anger from her face and, moving languidly, returns to couch, seats herself in her previous posture and returns her hand to* TOMASSO.)

TOMASSO (*indicating gramophone*). Do you *want* this?

(MARINA *becomes aware of the recurring music, rolls her eyes to heaven with a martyred look, sighs and rises.*)

(*Beginning to rise*) I'll do it.
MARINA (*wearily irritable*). Oh, never mind!

(TOMASSO *subsides, and lapses back into his abstraction.* MARINA *crosses to gramophone, snaps it off viciously, turns, re-assumes her languid air, returns to couch, sits in previous posture and returns her hand to* TOMASSO.)

MARINA (*off-handedly*). Yes—I suppose it's a bit of an up-heaval, in a way, but—these things will happen.
TOMASSO (*absently*). Hm!

MARINA.   It's no good crying over spilt milk, is it ?   (*Glances at him.*)

(TOMASSO *remains lost in thought.*)

After all, he's not irreplaceable, is he ?

(*Still no reply from* TOMASSO.)

(*Edging closer to him*) I mean, life has its compensations, hasn't it ?

(TOMASSO *remains oblivious.*)

(*Edging still closer*) I've still got you, for instance.

(*Still no reply.*)

(*A little louder*) I say, I've still got . . . (*Sharply.*)   Tomasso ! I'm *talk*ing to you.

TOMASSO.   Just a minute, dear—I'm thinking.

MARINA (*flaring up*).   Well, don't sit there thinking when I'm killing myself trying to be nice to you !

TOMASSO.   Marina !   (*Fumbles for pills.*)

MARINA (*rudely*).   What ?

TOMASSO (*rises and moves a few paces away*).   Marina—how would it be if—(*takes a pill*)—if I told you that—(*takes a pill*)—that I *know* this Mystery Man ?   (*Pauses.*)

(MARINA *rises and waits breathlessly.*)

And that he's not at all the romantic figure you seem to think he is.

MARINA.   Oh, I should be so happy.

TOMASSO.   Yes—quite !—Well, I don't know how to say it, Marina, but the fact is—it was I.   (*Hangs his head in deep shame.*)

MARINA (*triumphantly*).   Ah !

TOMASSO.   I can't explain it.   Perhaps it was pathological.   I can only say how deeply sorry I . . .

MARINA (*interrupting—excitedly moving towards archway*).   Get me a taxi, will you ?

TOMASSO (*astounded*).   I beg your pardon ?

MARINA.   Quickly, dear !

TOMASSO. Didn't you hear what I said ?

MARINA. Yes, of course I . . .

TOMASSO (*interrupting*). I'm telling you that I'm the Mystery Man—the rotten swine who's been . . .

MARINA (*interrupting*). Well, never mind about that now. You've been very naughty and we'll say no more about it. But you must do what you can to repair the damage you've done, you know.

TOMASSO. Oh, yes I . . .

MARINA (*interrupting*). Then go and get a taxi ! (*Turns for archway.*) I'll get a wrap.

TOMASSO. Just a minute, though !

(MARINA *halts.*)

What are you going to tell him if you catch him ?

MARINA (*regretfully*). Well—the truth !

TOMASSO. About *me* ?

MARINA. Well, yes ! You see, it's only the fact that it's *you* that makes the whole thing turn out to be so completely unimportant.

TOMASSO. Oh, I realise that, but . . . (*Hesitates.*)

MARINA. Perhaps you'd better go abroad for a bit.

TOMASSO. I wasn't thinking of *that* so much, only . . . (*Hesitates.*)

MARINA. Only what ?

TOMASSO. Isn't it going to make *you* look a bit silly ?

MARINA. How ?

TOMASSO. Having to admit that you got yourself into such a state over nothing more exciting than—me !

MARINA (*dismayed*). Oh !—Oh, dear !—I never *thought* of that. (*Coming slowly down again.*) How *dread*ful !

TOMASSO. So, I was thinking . . . (*Takes her arm.*)

MARINA. Yes ?

TOMASSO (*bringing her slowly down*). How would it be, if you told Alberto that—all this time—you'd believed it to be—him ?

MARINA. Believed it to be Alberto ?

TOMASSO. Yes.

MARINA. Who'd been sending the roses and writing the . . .

TOMASSO (*interrupting*). Yes.

MARINA. But, why on earth should I think he'd do a thing like that ?

Tomasso. To test you!

Marina. Test me?

Tomasso. Yes. You thought the Mystery Man was a sort of a trap.

Marina. Set for me?

Tomasso. Yes.

Marina. By Alberto?

Tomasso. Yes.

Marina. And not a real person at *all?*

Tomasso. No.

Marina. Then why did I fall in love with him?

Tomasso. You didn't!

Marina. Uh?

Tomasso. You only pre*tend*ed to.

Marina. What for?

Tomasso. To punish Alberto.

Marina (*catching on*). For setting the trap!

Tomasso. Exactly!

Marina. But, Tomasso, I think that's *bril*liant.

Tomasso. Good!

Marina. Because *that*'ll mean that *he*'ll be the one to look silly, won't it?

Tomasso. What about it, then?

Marina (*enthusiastically*). Oh, yes! *Yes!*

Tomasso. Right! Well—(*starts for* F.W.)—you don't want to miss him.

Marina (*calling*). Rosina!

Tomasso (*at* F.W.). You think out the details, and . . . (*Picks up his hat from cabinet.*)

Marina (*interrupting*). Yes, dear, and thank you! Thank you *so* much!

Tomasso. . . . and I'll get a taxi.

(*Exit* Tomasso, F.W.)

(*Enter* Rosina, L.)

Marina (*excitedly*). Rosina—we've had a *won*derful idea.

Rosina. What?

Marina. I'm *not* going to say it was Signor Savelli at *all*.

Rosina. You're not?

Marina. No, I'm going to say to my husband—" Alberto,

I'm *quite* well aware that *all* these flowers and things have been coming from *you.*"

ROSINA (*looking blank*). But they *haven't*!

MARINA. I *know* they haven't. (*Begins moving towards archway.*)

(ROSINA *follows.*)

But—don't you *see?*—When he *says* they haven't, *I* shall say— " Oh, *haven't* they, Alberto dear ? I'm *terribly* sorry. I've been under a misapprehension all this time."

ROSINA. Oh, I *see!*

(*Exit* MARINA *and* ROSINA (A.) *and to* R.)

MARINA (*off—laughing*). Isn't it a joy ?

ROSINA (*off*). So, by *that* means, you'll be able to . . .

MARINA (*off—laughing*). Yes !

(*Short pause. Enter* ALBERTO (A.) *from* L. *He wears his hat. He stamps in looking very irate, switches on main lights and at once begins hurriedly searching for something—lifting cushions, feeling in upholstery, etc. After a moment, he crosses towards desk. As he does so,* BERNARDO'S *whistle is heard, off.*)

ALBERTO (*changes his direction to* F.W., *leans out and bellows almost hysterically*). Shut-up ! (*Continues to desk, spots his wallet with a grunt of satisfaction, picks it up and turns away pocketing it.*)

(*Enter* MARINA *followed by* ROSINA (A.) *from* R. *They enter hurriedly, looking startled, and halt on seeing* ALBERTO. MARINA *carries a light coat.*)

MARINA. Oh !

ALBERTO (*crossing*). Left my blasted wallet !

MARINA (*interposes herself*). Just a minute !

ALBERTO (*halting behind couch*). I can't stop now, I'm . . .

MARINA (*interrupting*). I've something to say to you. It's important.

(ROSINA *moves down* L. *with excited backward glances.*)

(*Exit* ROSINA, L.)

ALBERTO.   Well ?

MARINA.   Alberto—I think you've been punished enough.

ALBERTO (*uncomprehendingly*).   I beg your pardon ?

MARINA.   Actually, I was on my way to the Station to stop you.   (*Indicates coat and throws it over back of chair*, L.C.)   I'd no intention of letting you *go*, you know.

ALBERTO (*bemused*).   You hadn't ?

MARINA (*going to him*).   Oh, no !   I was just leaving it until the last minute, that's all—to impress it on your mind.

ALBERTO.   Impress what on my mind ?

MARINA (*gently firm*).   That I'm not to be trifled with, Alberto dear.—However, as you *have* come back, we'll let that part go.—I think you've *learnt* your lesson.   (*Removes his hat, takes it* L. *and puts it on radio.*)

ALBERTO (*glances at his watch*).   Look !   Would you mind . . . ?

MARINA (*returning to him—interrupting*).   And this time—(*wags a warning finger*)—*this* time—I'm going to forgive you—though I needn't warn you—it mustn't happen again !—(*Takes his face in her two hands and kisses him.*)   Now !—Perhaps *you*'d like to say something !   (*Smiles, pats his face and moves away to mirror.*)

ALBERTO.   Er—before we go any further . . .   (*Breaks off.*)

MARINA (*dabbing complacently at her hair*).   Yes, dear ?

ALBERTO.   Would you mind making that a little clearer ?

MARINA.   Making what clearer ?

ALBERTO.   Exactly what I'm being forgiven *for !*

MARINA.   For sending me roses and writing me letters and pretending to be somebody else.

ALBERTO.   Oh !

MARINA.   I've known all along, you know.

ALBERTO.   Oh !   (*Walks slowly to couch and sits.*)

MARINA (*looking keenly at his reflection in the mirror*).   Alberto !

ALBERTO.   Yes ?

MARINA (*sharply*).   I say I've known from the beginning that . . .

ALBERTO (*interrupting*).   I know.   I heard you.

MARINA (*whips round*).   Well ?

(ALBERTO *avoids her eye and does not answer.*)

Haven't you anything to *say ?*

ALBERTO (*shrugs humbly*).   I can only say I'm sorry.

MARINA.   What *for?*

ALBERTO (*surprised*).   Well, for—for what you said I'd——

MARINA (*interrupting*).   But, aren't you going to deny it?

ALBERTO.   What's the good of denying it, if you know?

MARINA (*staggered*).   You—you mean it *was* you?

ALBERTO.   You've just *said* so.   What's the *matter* with you?

MARINA.   You—*cad!*

ALBERTO (*startled*).   Huh?

MARINA (*going to* L. *of couch*).   How *dare* you play such a trick on me?

ALBERTO (*bewildered*).   But . . .

MARINA (*interrupting*).   How *dare* you pass yourself off as a—as a—as a . . . (*Breaks off at a loss for a word.*)

ALBERTO (*plaintively*).   But, you just said you'd forgi . . .

MARINA (*interrupting*).   Setting *out* like that—de*li*berately—to hum*i*liate me!   *Try*ing to catch me out!   *Hop*ing to!   Hoping to make a *fool* of me!   I never *heard* of anything so contemptible.

ALBERTO (*morosely*).   Well, I've said I'm sorry.   I don't know what else I can do.

MARINA.   You can *catch* your beastly train.

ALBERTO.   I've lost it now, anyway.

MARINA.   Then get the next!   (*Throws herself into chair,* L.C.) I'm done with you.   (*Sits fuming.*)

ALBERTO (*ponders in puzzlement a second, then shakes his head.*) I don't get it.   (*Rises, walks upstage, pauses with back turned, thinking—then comes down to her.*)   Listen!—I don't quite understand this.—First you say I set a trap for you—then you say you forgive me—then, when I say I'm sorry, you fly into a temper and tell me to get the next train.—What's the idea?

(MARINA, *her head turned away, does not reply.*)

(*In sudden suspicion*).   *Did* you know, or were you only guessing?

MARINA.   Of *course* I knew.   You can't deceive a woman over a thing like that.   It's—it's intuitive.

ALBERTO.   All *right* then!   Was it all play-acting or wasn't it?

MARINA.   Was *what* all play-acting?

ALBERTO.   This *thing* of yours with the blasted Mystery Man?

MARINA.   Well, it *must* have been, mustn't it, you idiot?

ALBERTO.   Just to *pun*ish me?

MARINA. *Yes !*

ALBERTO. Well—*have* I been punished enough, or *have*n't I ?

(MARINA *does not reply.*)

And *do* you forgive me, or *not ?*

(MARINA *still remains silent.*)

I mean, *make* up your *mind.* I've got a *taxi* waiting.

MARINA (*ungraciously*). Well—if I said so—I suppose **I** must.

·ALBERTO. You *do* forgive me ?

MARINA. I suppose so.

ALBERTO. That's definite ?

MARINA. Certainly—if I say so.

ALBERTO. No misunderstanding about it ?

MARINA. No.

ALBERTO. Right ! Thanks very much ! (*Goes to couch and throws himself sullenly into it.*)

(MARINA *regards him for a moment and her expression softens. She rises and moves behind couch.*)

MARINA (*gently*). To be honest, though—it wasn't en*tire*ly play-acting.

(ALBERTO *looks up questioningly.*)

He *was* rather sweet, you know.

ALBERTO (*faintly indignant*). Well, he was *meant* to be.

MARINA. And I *did* love him—in a way.

ALBERTO. What do you mean " in a way " ?

MARINA. Well—in a way that I never loved *you.*

ALBERTO. But it *was* me.

MARINA. I know. That's what's so odd about it.

ALBERTO. What's odd about that ? I can be glamorous, you know, if I want to.

MARINA. But you don't seem to want to.

ALBERTO. There's no call for it in the ordinary course of events.

MARINA (*Comes swiftly round couch and sits beside him*). But it's such a *sin* to waste a gift like that.

ALBERTO. Huh ?

MARINA. To me, there was something—almost holy about that man.

ALBERTO (*gratified*). Really ?

MARINA. His *letters*, Alberto . . . !

ALBERTO (*smugly*). They weren't bad, were they—in their way ?

MARINA. They were the letters of a—*prince.*

ALBERTO. Think so ?

MARINA (*gazing into his face*). Alberto—you could be so wonderful.

ALBERTO (*swelling slightly*). So you think it's a sort of a gift, do you—like painting or singing—that *ought* to be given to the world ?

MARINA (*moving a little closer to him*). Not to the *world*, dear !

ALBERTO (*largely*). Well—so long as you've got me, there's no reason why you shouldn't have this other chap too, if you want him.

MARINA. A sort of two-in-one, you mean ?

ALBERTO. In a way, yes.

MARINA (*snuggling to him*). Oh, that 'ud be lovely, Alberto.

ALBERTO (*puts an arm round her and kisses her on top of the head*). So you do pretty well out of it, don't you ?

MARINA. Yes—I do pretty well out of it.

(MARINA *sighs, closes her eyes, and remains clinging to him in deep content. For a moment they remain blissfully thus.*)

ALBERTO. I say !

MARINA. Um ?

ALBERTO. I've still got that damn taxi out there.

MARINA (*disengaging and sitting up—disappointedly*). Oh—Alberto ! *He* would *never* have said that.

ALBERTO. Ah, but I was thinking—why don't we go somewhere ?

MARINA (*without enthusiasm*). In the taxi ?

ALBERTO (*pleased with himself*). Yes.

MARINA. Now ?

ALBERTO. Yes. Supper or something !

MARINA. Isn't it rather late ?

ALBERTO. Now, look here ! Do you want this two-in-one business, or not ?

MARINA. Of course, but . . .

ALBERTO (*seizing her wrist, rising, dragging her after him to chair, L.C.*). Then get your coat on ! (*Grabbing coat and holding it for her.*) It's not going to be en*tire*ly one-sided, you know. I've got to have *some*thing to work on.

(MARINA *slips into the coat, catches his hands and holds his arms round her.*)

MARINA. I a*dore* you when you're masterful.

(ALBERTO'S *expression softens. He bends his head and kisses her on the side of the neck.*)
(*Calling*) Rosina !
ALBERTO (*still holding her—with a grin*). You know—I'm going to enjoy telling Tomasso about this.
MARINA. *Dear* Tomasso ! (*Suddenly becomes thoughtfully puzzled.*)
ALBERTO. He thinks I don't understand women.

(*Enter* ROSINA (L.).)

ROSINA (*at door*). Yes, Signora ?
ALBERTO. We're going out for a bit. (*Releases* MARINA, *picks up his hat and goes up to archway.*)
ROSINA. Yes, Signor !

(*Exit* ROSINA, L.)

(MARINA *remains standing in puzzled thought.*)

ALBERTO. What are you waiting for ?
MARINA. When you mentioned Tomasso just now, I got the strangest feeling that—I'd forgotten something.
ALBERTO. Oh, never mind about that now ! Come on ! (*Holds out his hand to her.*)

(MARINA *gives it up with a shrug, goes to him and takes his hand.*)

MARINA. Where did you think of going ?
ALBERTO. *Plaza* ! Where do *you* think ?

(*They both laugh.*)

MARINA. Darling ! (*Kisses him.*)

(*Exeunt* ALBERTO *and* MARINA (A.) *and to* L.)

(*Instantly* BERNARDO'S *face appears at window up* R., *looks in and passes on.*

Enter BERNARDO, F. W. *Grinning, he carries a posy. Moving swiftly and cautiously, he tip-toes to coffee-table, puts posy on it and returns to* F. W. *In the act of stepping outside, he stops abruptly, then turns, looks about him in panic, darts across and secretes himself behind the wall at* R. *side of archway.*

Enter TOMASSO, F. W.

Breathless and with his hat in his hand he comes in looking round expectantly.)

TOMASSO (*calling*). Marina ! (*Throws his hat into couch and goes up to archway.*) Marina ! I've got your cab. It's at the side gate.

(*Enter* ROSINA, L.)

ROSINA. Oh, they're just going out, Signor Savelli.
TOMASSO. They ?
ROSINA. Yes. The Signor came back.
TOMASSO. Oh, I see !—Was there any message, Rosina ?
ROSINA. No Signor ! Should there have been ?
TOMASSO (*with no hint of resentment or self-pity*). There might have been.
ROSINA. Perhaps they forgot.
TOMASSO. Yes—perhaps they forgot.

(*Front door slams, off.*)

ROSINA. Shall I get you some coffee, or something ?
TOMASSO (*moving to couch*). No. No, thank you, Rosina !
I think I'll just . . . (*Breaks off and picks up his hat. As he begins to turn away, he sees posy.*) What's this ? (*Comes round and picks it up.*) An orchid, eh ?
ROSINA (*going to him in sudden alarm*). An orchid ?
TOMASSO. Looks like it !

ROSINA.   In *lot*us leaves ?
TOMASSO.   Could be !
ROSINA.   Then I—I think it's for *me*.

(TOMASSO *makes to hand it to her.*)

ROSINA (*drawing away*).   Oh, but I don't *want* it.
TOMASSO.   Oh !   (*Smiles, drops posy on to coffee-table, turns and gently pinches her cheek.*)   Nice child !   (*Goes slowly and rather forlornly to archway.*)   Take care of yourself, Rosina !
ROSINA.   Oh, I *will*, Signor Savelli !
TOMASSO (*nods and smiles*).   Good-night !   (*Puts on his hat and goes out.*)

(*Exit* TOMASSO (A.) *and to* L.)

(ROSINA *immediately runs to French-windows, closes them, locks and bolts them.   While she is doing so,* BERNARDO, *grinning wickedly, emerges from his hiding place.*)

CURTAIN

THE END

STAGE PLAN THROUGHOUT THE PLAY

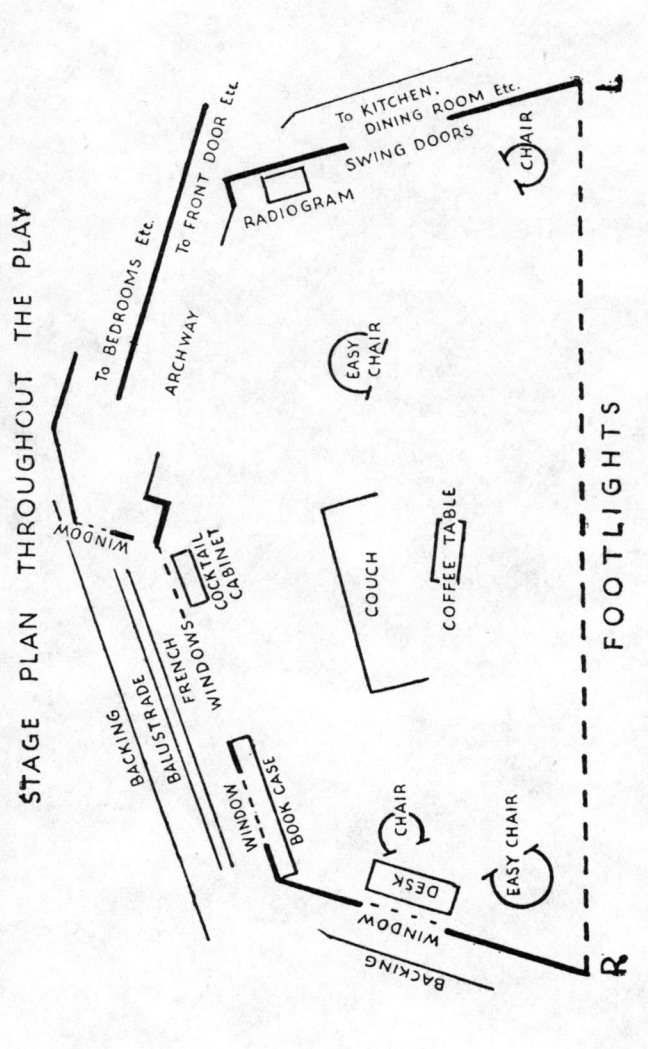

FOOTLIGHTS

PROPERTY PLOT

ON STAGE.

Under window R.   Desk (with drawers) bearing blotter, ink-stand, fountain pen, ashtray, magazines, telephone, lamp. In top L. drawer of desk—luggage labels and cards. All drawers filled with papers.

At desk.   Elbow chair.

Back R.   Bookcase. (Some books practical.)

Up L.   Radiogram with cupboard containing records.

Above radio.   Mirror.

R.C.   Couch with two cushions.

Below couch.   Low coffee-table bearing cigarette box, Italian magazines, ashtray, box of matches.

L.C.   Easy chair with cushion.

Down R.   Small easy chair with cushion.

Down L.   Elbow chair.

Back C.   Cabinet or table with drinks. Whisky, gin, vermouth, glasses, etc. Lamp and ashtray on cabinet.

OFF STAGE R.

Posy of purple tulip and laurel leaves. (Bernardo.)
Bouquet of red roses. (Bernardo.)
Posy of red rose, white rose and ivy. (Bernardo.)
Bunch of very dilapidated red roses.
Posy of orchid and lotus leaves. (Bernardo.)

OFF STAGE L.

Letter envelope. (Marina.)
Golf bag with clubs. (Alberto.)
One golf shoe. (Alberto.)
Soft felt hat. (Alberto.)
Italian railway guide. (Marina.)
Two sandwiches. (Alberto and Tomasso.)
Vase containing roses. (Rosina.)
Pair of vases on pedestals.
Tall vase.
Two smaller vases.
Tray with tea-things. (Rosina.)
Bunch of six dozen red roses. (Rosina.)
Brief-case. (Alberto.)
Several books. (Rosina.)
Several ties. (Rosina.)
Hot-water bottle. (Rosina.)
Hold-all. (Alberto.)

Tennis racket in frame.   (Alberto.)
Pneumatic cushion.   (Alberto.)
Shooting stick.   (Alberto.)
Rug.   (Alberto.)
Umbrella.   (Alberto.)
Small bag.   (Alberto.)
Raincoat.   (Alberto.)
Hat.   (Alberto.)
Small suitcase half filled with books and papers.
Large suitcase full of clothes.
Pile of shirts.

PERSONAL PROPERTIES.

TOMASSO.   Diary, pencil, watch, hat, walking-stick
    Italian banknotes, bottle of pills.
MARINA.   Compact and lipstick.
ALBERTO.   Wrist-watch and wallet.

DURING FIRST INTERVAL.

Put fountain-pen in bottom L. drawer of desk.
Strike railway guide and sandwich.
Change magazines.
Change roses on desk for old ones.
Wash glasses.
Take bouquet from P. to O.P.
(Note.   Record used for effect during Act II—Columbia
    LX 824.   " Les Toreadors.")

DURING SECOND INTERVAL.

Strike elbow chair, down L.
Desk very untidy—drawers open—papers on top.
Alberto's jacket over back of chair L.C.
Small suitcase (open) on back of couch.
Large suitcase (open) on floor down R.
Pile of shirts over back of couch.
Fresh roses in vase on desk.
Loose roses spread on coffee-table.
Pedestals with vases dressed with roses on either side
    of archway.
Tall vase dressed with roses, on floor down L.
Small vase dressed with roses on cabinet.
Small vase dressed with roses on ledge of window,
    back R.
French-windows open.
Window curtains drawn.
All light fittings on.
(Note.   Record used for effect during Act III—
    H.M.V., B.D.5995.   " No Greater Love.")

INHERIT THE WIND

A Play in Three Acts

By JEROME LAWRENCE and ROBERT E. LEE

16 male, 5 female, One Composite Set

"A rare and stimulating experience."—
Evening Standard.

THE SHOP AT SLY CORNER

A Play in Three Acts

By EDWARD PERCY

6 male, 4 female, One Set

"Mr. Percy is a craftsman with a conscience, his play excels London's recent thrillers. This is a profitable appointment with fear."—*Punch.*

WANTED, ONE BODY!

A Farcical Thriller in Three Acts

By RAYMOND DYER

5 male, 4 female, One Set

"Wanted, one Body . . . with murder and laughs galore was a hit!"—*Daily Herald.*

A SENSE OF GUILT

A Drama in Three Acts

By ANDREW ROSENTHAL

3 male, 5 female, One Set

"A superb theme."—*Lancashire Evening Post.*

ONE OF THE FAMILY

A Comedy in Three Acts

By CHARLES CAMERON

7 female, 3 male, One Set

A topical domestic comedy—full of laughs and fun.

BASINFUL OF THE BRINY

A Comedy in Three Acts

By LESLIE SANDS

3 male, 6 female, One Set

A riotous follow-up to the sensationally successful
" Beside the Seaside."

BLACK CHIFFON

A Play in Three Acts

By LESLEY STORM

4 female, 3 male, One Set

" This is an exciting and absorbing play."—*Punch*

THE SECRET TENT

A Play in Three Acts

By ELIZABETH ADDYMAN

4 female, 3 male, One Set

" It has some of the most tantalizing curtains ever
invented, leaving the audience aching for the intervals
to end."—*Daily Express*.

BESIDE THE SEASIDE

A Comedy in Three Acts

By LESLIE SANDS

6 female, 3 male, 1 set

" It is one huge laugh from beginning to end. "—*Herald & Express, Torquay.*

WATERS OF THE MOON

A Comedy in Three Acts

By N. C. HUNTER

6 female, 4 male, 1 set

" A play of unmistakable quality."—*Evening News.*

A LADY MISLAID

A Comedy in Three Acts

By KENNETH HORNE

3 male, 4 female, 1 set

" Here is a civilized and charming evening."—*Observer.*